Pull up a Chair

Pull up a Chair
southern company, conversations & cuisine

Published by The Junior League of Columbus, Georgia, Inc.
Copyright © 2010

The Junior League of Columbus, Georgia, Inc.
700 Broadway
Columbus, Georgia 31901
jlcolumbus.com
706.327.4207

Cover Art and Chair Sketches: © Erin Fitzhugh Gregory
Black-and-White Photography: © Olivia Cheves Blanchard
Food Photography: © Mike Culpepper Studios

Eames® is a registered trademark of Herman Miller, Inc.
The Eames® Chair represented on the cover and in the interior of
this book is a fully licensed product of Herman Miller, Inc.

This cookbook is a collection of favorite recipes, which are not
necessarily original recipes.

Library of Congress Control Number: 2009924209
ISBN: 978-0-9606300-2-8

Edited, Designed, and Produced by

||| Favorite Recipes® Press

an imprint of

FRP. INC

a wholly owned subsidiary of Southwestern/Great American, Inc.
P.O. Box 305142
Nashville, Tennessee 37230
800.358.0560

Editorial Director: Mary Cummings
Art Director and Book Design: Steve Newman
Project Manager: Debbie Van Mol
Editor: Linda Jones

Manufactured in the United States of America
First Printing: 2010
25,000 copies

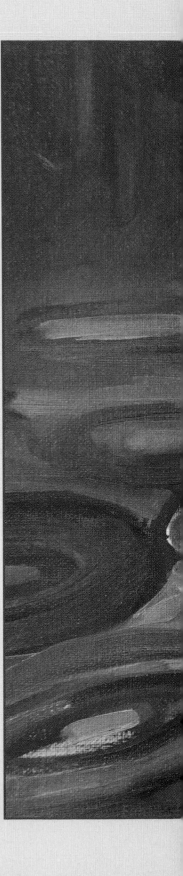

Pull up a Chair

southern company, conversations & cuisine

The Junior League of Columbus, Georgia

Mission

The Junior League of Columbus, Georgia, Inc., is an organization of women committed
to promoting volunteerism, developing the potential of women, and improving communities
through the effective action and leadership of trained volunteers.
Its purpose is exclusively educational and charitable.

Focus and Community Involvement

The League currently includes a membership of active and sustaining members of
over 750 dedicated women. Our active members give over 7,500 hours of volunteer service to
the community each year. In addition to our time, we have also contributed almost $2 million
to the community in our focus areas since inception. Over the years, the Junior League of Columbus
has been instrumental in many worthwhile projects that make our community a better place.
Some of those projects include the following:

Educating local elementary students on the dangers of drugs through the
Say No Gang Puppet Program

Sponsoring Kids in the Kitchen for our local partner in education, Wynnton Elementary School

Renovating the Columbus Museum's Transformation Room for young children

Promoting Children's Vision Screening at local elementary schools

Opening the doors at the Attic Sale for over fifty years

Helping to establish the local Ronald McDonald House

We will continue this legacy of service and commitment to our community as we
go forward in the future, focusing on the adoption of our signature issue, "The Healthy Child,"
promoting child health and well-being with a focus on both prevention and treatment.
For a child to be healthy, he or she must be protected, taught proper nutrition, educated,
have a positive mentor, have an advocate, and must have access to quality health care.
We want to help make our community a place where children are healthier and happy.

Preface

Our journey began on an abnormally cool day in May heading south from Nashville en route to Columbus from a cookbook conference. We were excited but apprehensive as our publisher encouraged us to "go out on a limb," in being creative and different. It was a refreshing, yet daunting charge, since our previous cookbooks are so well loved. We were eager to be distinctive, yet lost as to where to begin, which ran parallel with our navigational direction—lost. Thankfully, the additional time in the car helped to spark our meager attempts at development: we discussed trees, hats, windows, buildings, famous local cooks, and river themes, initially. Our ideas were as directionally challenged as our car. Finally, as we neared Highway 27, which would eventually take us home, the idea of *chairs* came to fruition.

This theme would allow us to marry the ideas culminated by both physical and emotional nutrition. You may pull up a chair to a table, but not to just any table, nor a table in the literal sense. You may pull together several blankets to enjoy a family picnic of tomato sandwiches in the park. You may pull up a "camp" chair to enjoy Buffalo wings with fellow fans while tailgating—anxiously anticipating the "big game." You may pull up a chair to a breakfast table with fresh blueberry pancakes calling your name, while hearing of the upcoming day's events, or a well-loved grandmother's tale of her first day at school. You may pull up a chair on Thanksgiving Day to an elegantly decorated table, hoping that you will remember every good laugh and every story, but knowing that you probably won't and therefore should savor every moment as much as every delectable bite. During these occasions, we are nourishing not only the body, but also the soul, as our emotional benefit is just as important these days as our physical nourishment.

Whatever the event, chairs are an integral part of each of our lives. Thus we have included a collection of well-loved chairs that are community favorites. Some are iconic, inspiring memories for continuing generations; others are unique to a family or a particular location. All are represented by the famous Eames® chair on our cover, openly welcoming and enveloping its occupants, offering them a sense of security, warmth, and generosity. These are the feelings that the Junior League of Columbus, Georgia, aspires to render through positive contributions and engagement within our community.

Thank you to our talented and hard-working committee, to their families, and especially to Carson, Hatch, Putt, Glenn, Ellie, and Sara Lanier, who somehow managed to pull up their own chairs to a meal when "Mama" couldn't be there during the development of this book. Our hectic lifestyles have in some sense diminished our gathering time. People rarely sit for hours around the dinner table talking and sharing. *Pull up a Chair*, the title of our cookbook, pays tribute to our belief that some of life's most cherished memories are created while enjoying good company, conversations, and cuisine.

Millie Peacock Patrick   Gardiner Zollo Church

Table of Contents

Pull up a Chair

Our Heritage recipes are designated with a bull's-eye.

Pull up a Chair

Introduction

"Columbus is the exquisite taste of peach ice cream fresh from the freezer," Charter Junior League of Columbus member Minnie Bullock Huston said in a 1974 presentation. "Columbus is biting into a rolled wafer, delicate and fragile, the sculpture of patient hands. It is cheese straws crisp and sharp kept ready by a cheerful friend who dispenses good humor with every daintily wrapped package. Columbus is Sunday worship in handsome churches followed by Sunday dinner enjoyed in family groups where the generation gap vanishes over the abundant food." Her words capture the essence of the nourishment that can be provided by food and the love of friends and family.

Today's families have many choices for food: dining out, driving through, picking up, or ordering in. Although these options are a helpful accommodation to the fast pace of life, there is no substitute for the type of nourishment that comes from lingering with good company over a delicious home-cooked meal. *Pull up a Chair*, the title of our cookbook, pays tribute to our belief that some of life's most cherished memories are created at the dinner table.

Pull up a Chair is the seventh cookbook created by the Junior League of Columbus, Georgia. The first, compiled in the early 1930s by the Community Service League, which later became the Junior League of Columbus, contains delicious Southern standards like fried chicken, cheese biscuits, and hand-churned lemon ice cream. First Lady Eleanor Roosevelt, an early member of the Junior League of New York City and an occasional neighbor at the Little White House in Warm Springs, Georgia, contributed four recipes.

The Junior League of Columbus published its second cookbook in 1957, with an updated edition in 1966. With talented editors Loulie Young Watson, Margaret Flournoy Bickerstaff, and Rebecca Pearce Gilbert, and a charming cover designed by architect Edward Neal, these cookbooks stand the test of time. International dishes like Cuban Arroz Amarillo, Bitochki and Pilaf, and Crepes Hotel Alois Lang appear alongside Squash Casserole and Mama's Blackberry Cobbler, hinting at the expanding palate of a more worldly local society. With the infantry school at Fort Benning as part of our community, national and international dishes naturally found their way into the repertoire of Columbus hostesses.

In 1979, a new cookbook, *A Southern Collection*, with Nancy Hodges Callaway and Ruth Combs Flowers serving as editors, met immediate success. During three printings, thirty thousand cookbooks found their way into the kitchens of eager cooks. As a tribute to the 1957 and 1966 books, favorite recipes were reprinted and marked with a pineapple, the symbol of hospitality. Tested three times before gaining admission onto the book's pages, each recipe promised and delivered a pleasing result. For new, aspiring hostesses, the italicized comments under the titles of certain recipes were like magnets: for preparing Creole Shrimp, you could *reap the compliments*. When presenting Tenderloin with Béarnaise to your waiting guests, you would *listen to the raves*. Visions of large dinner parties danced in the head of many a young bride who turned the pages. Shrimp Spread was guaranteed to be a *snap* and Brandy Flip Sherbet would be a *fun finale*. Having the name of the contributor printed neatly under the recipe provided an added enticement. Knowing that Mrs. Fabulous Cook III had donated the recipe made the dish even more desirable for one's table. Understandably, this book is a treasured possession. Occasionally, a copy will appear on eBay, but it is quickly snapped up by a wise shopper.

In the early 1980s, W. C. Bradley Enterprises, Incorporated, a historic Columbus business and manufacturer of Char-Broil grills, approached the Junior League of Columbus with the idea of an outdoor cookbook. In 1985, under the leadership of the W. C. Bradley Company and a Junior League committee headed by food editors Sheri Boykin Lawler and Betsy Blanchard Staples, the *Char-Broil Grill Lovers Cookbook* was published. This cookbook is a standard for outdoor entertaining and contains mouth-watering recipes that appeal to all ages.

In 1994, *A Southern Collection—Then and Now* made its premiere. Susan Hickey Mitchell and Lu Ann Binns Brandon, chairman and co-chairman, led the production of a cookbook by the Junior League of Columbus to a new level of sophistication. The handsome green and white cover with the photograph of a beloved antebellum home, St. Elmo, sets the stage for the combination of old and new recipes, menus with appropriate wine choices, and beautiful color photographs of Columbus landmarks. Again, the pineapple symbol is used to mark recipes from prior cookbooks: classics Chicken Tetrazzini and Mrs. Storey's Boiled Custard appear alongside new and delicious recipes like Snappy Cheese Wafers and Stir-Fry Chicken and Vegetables. Serve Banana Nut Cake and you will *listen to the raves*. The book is pretty enough to adorn a coffee table but is too helpful in the kitchen to remain there for long. *A Southern Collection—Then and Now* is in its fourth printing, a testament to its success.

In these excellent cookbooks, the Junior League of Columbus has paid homage to the fact that the preparation and presentation of delicious meals to family and friends is at the center of our culture. *Pull up a Chair* continues in this tradition. On the pages that follow, our best cooks share their favorite recipes for all types of occasions. Humorous and touching anecdotes are included as a tribute to our belief that the best meals are shared with good company. Asking you to pull up a chair at our table— be it casual or formal—and to share in the delicious dishes prepared in our kitchens is an invitation into our lives. Warm hospitality, a characteristic of life in the South, never goes out of style. We welcome you. Enjoy!

Mimi Pease Childs
President, 1985–1986

Foreword

For those of us raised in the South, food and entertaining are central themes in our lives, past and present. Something in our DNA gives us the ability—and desire—to make people feel welcome. Whether we've known a friend since the dawn of time, or we've just met a person on the street corner, cheese biscuits and iced tea emerge on their arrival, with perhaps an invitation to stay for supper. It's a subtle communication of, "Let's get to know each other better. Tell me what's on your mind."

With *Pull up a Chair: Southern Company, Conversations and Cuisine*, the Junior League of Columbus has expertly captured the mystique of Southern hospitality. In the pages following, exquisite photos will draw you into familiar settings showcasing fabulous recipes from traditional Southern favorites like mint juleps and blueberry pie to a fresh interpretation of a well-stuffed tomato. Useful tips on setting a knockout table will help novice and seasoned hosts alike to update their style. I'm personally inspired to take things out of the dining room and into the outdoors for my next dinner party!

Finally, the stories and anecdotes throughout the book will give you good reason to take to your favorite chair, prop up your feet, and relax after all your hard work in the kitchen.

Enjoy!

Tara Guérard

Tara Guérard's Tips for a Perfect Table

1. Always press your table linens and napkins before use—no fold lines allowed!

2. Remember that flower centerpieces or table arrangements should not be so large that they interfere with table conversations—your guests should be able to see one another above and around the arrangements. Also, you can never have too many candles and votives. Everyone looks better in candlelight!

3. Choose unexpected glassware for a more modern table; use stemless wine glasses, for example, or tumblers to serve water and wine.

4. Do not pre-pour ice water into glasses—the glass or sterling will sweat and water dripping down the stemware will result in a ring or wet spot on the table linen. Even worse, it will damage a wooden table.

5. Handwritten menus, even for the smallest, most intimate dinner party, are a wonderful detail to add. Select a special card and create a menu (with wines) for each place setting.

Sponsors

GOLD

Synovus Financial Corp.

SILVER

Amos-Cheves Foundation, Inc.

BMW of Columbus

Mr. and Mrs. John W. Walden, Jr.

Schomburg Jewelers
In honor of Millie Peacock Patrick, Laura Schomburg Patrick,
Lee Schomburg Kent, and Nelia Schomburg Partain
In memory of Marilee Nuckolls Schomburg and Caroline Nuckolls Flournoy

W. C. Bradley Co.

Acura of Columbus

Columbus Bank and Trust

TSYS

J. Smith Lanier

Pezold Management Group

Donna Brown, Sallie Martin, and Marie Moshell
In honor of Sue Marie Thompson Turner

Dell Caldwell, Clara Middlebrooks, Mac Turner, and Hooper Turner, Jr.
In honor of Dell McMath Turner

Sponsors

BRONZE

Margaret Amos, Frances Berry,
Lynn Grogan, Libbie Key,
Linda Logan, Genie Mize,
Kelly Pridgen, Margie Richardson,
Sharon Sanders, and Cindy Sparks
> In honor of Junior League
> presidents—past, present,
> and future

Ben's Chophouse

Colleen Rustin
> In honor of Sandra Day,
> Stacey Boyd, and Mary Boyd
> In memory of
> Mildred Byrd Rustin

Corrin Riley
> In honor of Kathy J. Riley

Dinglewood Pharmacy

Hinson Galleries, Inc.
> In honor of Dradyn C. Hinson
> and Jeanie Hinson Bross

Jennifer Batson Cooley
> In honor of
> Margaret Neal Amos

Mary S. Boyd
> In honor of Jennifer Boyd,
> Julie Boyd, and Stacey Boyd

Merett Alexander

Carson and Hatch Patrick
> In honor of
> Millie Peacock Patrick

Mr. and Mrs. Madden Hatcher, Jr.
> In honor of Mrs. Sam Dismuke
> In memory of
> Mrs. Neill Bickerstaff (Sara)
> and Mrs. Madden Hatcher
> (Sue Mac)

Kathy J. Riley
> In honor of Corrin W. Riley

Mr. and Mrs. Sam Dismuke
> In honor of Mrs. James
> Madden Hatcher, Jr., and
> Mrs. John Douglas Poshon
> In memory of Mrs. Frederick
> Wynne Dismuke,
> Mrs. Lindsay Neill Bickerstaff,
> and Mrs. J. Madden Hatcher

Mrs. Richard Y. Bradley

Mrs. Carol Turner Flournoy
> In honor of
> Mrs. Kelly Flournoy Pridgen

Mrs. Olivia Cheves Blanchard
> In honor of
> Bettye Amos Cheves

Mrs. William Bryan Hardegree, Jr.
> In memory of
> Mrs. Carter Woolfolk

Stacey Boyd

The Columbus Museum

Tires First
> In honor of Jackie Hargrove

Alexander Contracting Co., Inc.

Alexander Electric Co.
> In honor of Robin Grier

Margaret G. Zollo
> In honor of Gardiner Z. Church

Alan, Jake, and Luke Snipes
> In honor of Michele Snipes

Buford's Brownies

Tom Flowers
> In honor of
> Loretta Sparrow Flowers

Greg, Wil, and Shelby Wells
> In honor of Joy Wells

Daniel Appliance Co.

Livingston Storage & Transfer
> In honor of
> Jaime Davis Livingston

Mary Bradley, Margaret
McCormick, Sally Bradley,
and Vandy Middleton
> In memory of
> Margaret Flournoy Bickerstaff

Jarrell Palmer Schley and
Jennings Adams DeWitt Palmer
> In honor of Mrs. J. Daniel
> Palmer, Nancy Jarrell
> Hardaway Schley, and
> Margaret O'Neal Lewis
> In memory of
> Dr. J. Daniel Palmer

Billy, Russell, Betsy, and
Walter Blanchard
> In honor of
> Olivia Cheves Blanchard

Elizabeth Ogie, Polly Miller,
Kate Wilson, Abby Irby,
and Susan Wainwright
> In honor of Betty Corn

In honor of Nancy Callaway from
> her children

The 2008–2009 Provisional Class

Cordy Wiley Arnold and Bolts Wiley
> In memory of Carson B. Wiley
> and Jane B. Wiley

Lane and Chandler Riley

Gardiner Church
> In honor of the *Pull up a Chair*
> Cookbook Committee

Gardiner Church
> In honor of Margaret Glenn
> Zollo, Eleanor Glenn Hardegree,
> and Hilda Hughes Church

Barber, Robert, and Kight Wilson
> In honor of Tiffany Wilson

Sponsors

CONTRIBUTOR

Fitzgerald Bickerstaff
In honor of Margie Bickerstaff

Mrs. Shriver J. Tommey

Bob, Maylyn, and Robert Hinson
In honor of Dradyn C. Hinson

Mr. and Mrs. Joseph C. Bross, Jr.
In honor of Dradyn C. Hinson

Wendi Jenkins
In honor of Shari Milam

Ashley S. Turner
In honor of Glenda L. Sexton and
Sally L. Turner

Emily Trotter
In memory of Joyce Hess

Glenwood School, Inc.

Janice P. Biggers

Jill and Andy Philips
In memory of
Mary Louise Duffee Philips

Margaret and Bo Ward
In honor of McClain and
Park Ward

Mrs. Britney Stahl

Donna S. Hand
In honor of Gardiner Church

Vance and Kimberly Beck

Burt's Butcher Shoppe

Containers by Reaves

Meredith L. King
In honor of Mrs. Larry A. King
and Miss Julie A. King
In memory of Mrs. James R. Self

Kee, Tripp, and Parks Evans
In honor of Edie Evans

Lori Turner

Beth Kirven
In memory of Shirley A. Kirven
and Ella E. Kirven

Mary Lou Jarrell

Millie Peacock Patrick
In honor of the *Pull up a Chair*
Cookbook Committee

Jay Bross
In honor of Jeanie Hinson Bross

Glenn, Ellie, and Sara Lanier Church
In honor of
Gardiner Zollo Church

Lucy and Rand Jones
In honor of Dori Sponcler Jones

Ms. Amelia A. Vaught
In honor of Kathryn S. Vaught
and Kathryn V. Roberts

Butler's Pantry

The Bridge Club children
In honor of Mrs. James W. Key

Brian, Rachel, and Riley Grier
In honor of
Robin Alexander Grier

Tyler Bickerstaff
In honor of Shannan Hartley
Bickerstaff

Michelle Hudson

Tracy Gay
In honor of Wendy Gay

John and Bo Patterson
In memory of Dot Patterson

Elinor Martin Harper and
Lucy Martin Jackson
In honor of Nancy Martin

Mary-Tom West Paris
In memory of Mrs. Richard
Newcomb West, Sr.

Jaime and Scott Livingston
In honor of Davis, Isa, and
David-Scott Livingston

Acknowledgments

Erin Fitzhugh Gregory

Erin (cover painting and sketch artist) is a native of Mobile, Alabama, and currently resides in Columbus, Georgia, with her husband, Tim, and their daughter, McCall.

Since graduating from Auburn University in 2000 with a B.F.A in painting, Erin has made her love of art a full-time career. While selling her paintings in multiple galleries throughout the Southeast, she also spends much of her time doing commissioned work and has done several book-illustrating projects. In addition to creating art, Erin also enjoys teaching oil painting workshops.

Erin's passion for painting is reflected in her rich, colorful landscapes, still-lifes, and figurative paintings. Her objective is to capture the contrasting nature of sunlight and shadow, and to bring it to life with vivid color and brushwork.

Erin has received numerous awards for her art and has been featured in various regional magazines. Since 2001, she has had several solo shows and her paintings have been featured in multiple exhibitions around the Southeast. Learn more about her art at her Web site, www.efgart.com/biography.html. She is an active member of the Junior League of Columbus.

Olivia Cheves Blanchard

Olivia (photographer) is a native of Columbus, Georgia, and currently resides in Columbus with her husband, Billy, and their three children, Russell, Betsy, and Walter. She is a graduate of the University of Georgia with a bachelor's degree in journalism as a magazine major with a photography concentration. Olivia enjoys painting and photography as creative outlets. "Anytime you are able to use your time and talents to serve a cause larger than yourself, you are always the one that ends up receiving the blessing."

Olivia is an active member of the Junior League of Columbus.

Tara Guérard
Founder and President, Soirée by Tara Guérard

Recognized as the Southeast's premier event designer, Tara Guérard has earned a national reputation for her exceptional ability to create spectacular settings celebrating life's most anticipated occasions. Clients across the United States—from celebrity hosts to hometown brides—seek out Tara for her signature Southern graciousness infused with a decidedly modern flair.

Since opening the doors of Soirée by Tara Guérard in Charleston, South Carolina, over a decade ago, Tara has been noted as a leading arbiter of entertaining and Southern style. In 2005, she was selected as a Top 25 Trendsetter by *Modern Bride* magazine. Soirée's work has also been featured by a wide range of media, including *Elegant Bride, Food & Wine, Grace Ormonde Wedding Style, Martha Stewart Weddings, InStyle Weddings,* and *Town & Country Weddings,* among other prestigious publications. Most recently, Tara was tapped by Martha Stewart and the editors of *Martha Stewart Weddings* to create a "Gorgeous and Green" Nashville, Tennessee, wedding that was highlighted in the magazine and televised on the Style network in December 2008.

Tara's debut lifestyle book, *Southern Weddings: New Looks from the Old South* (Gibbs Smith), was published to rave reviews in early 2007, and a follow-up volume is planned for 2010. Tara lives in the historic district of Charleston with her husband, Russell, their son, Aiken, and springer spaniel Georgia. For additional information and to view a selection of Tara's events, please visit www.soireecharleston.com.

Cookbook Committee

Chair	Millie Peacock Patrick
Chair	Gardiner Zollo Church
Treasurer	Amelia Alcorn Vaught
Recipe Chair	Edie Pendleton Evans
Recipe Co-Chair	Robin Alexander Grier
Recipe Testing Chair	Dradyn Coolik Hinson
Non-Recipe Text Chair	Joy Bowick Wells
Marketing Chair	Whitney Rice Pease
Marketing Co-Chair	Kristi Kimmell Casto
Pre-Sales Chair	Jennifer Calamusa Adams
Pre-Sales Co-Chair	Sara Stola Evans
Sponsorship Chair	Merett McWhorter Alexander
Sponsorship Co-Chair	Crystal Angela Wing
Art & Design	Sara Hatcher Dismuke
Photographer	Olivia Cheves Blanchard
Food Stylist	SaSa Walden Bickerstaff
Artist	Erin Fitzhugh Gregory

Cookbook Subcommittees

Non-Recipe Text

Kristin Edmonson Campbell
Resa Pate Carter
Jensen Mast Melton

Caroline Garland Castle
Mitchi McKnight Wade

Testers

Shelly Mathews Blanton
Laurie Nester Brinegar
Lisa Spafford Brown
Jennifer Wright Cooper
Beth Rauch Cutshall
Teresa Carswell Howard

Marietta Rushton O'Neill
Jennings Adams DeWitt Palmer
Mollie Morton Smith
Shriver Jones Tommey
Allison Weaver Peak
Chris Wagner Williams

Recipe Section Chairs

Appetizers & Beverages
Jennifer Ellington Walker

Grill & Game
Kelly Bladen McKinstry

Breakfast & Breads
Shannan Hartley Bickerstaff

Vegetables & Sides
Wendy Ryan Gay

Soups, Salads & Sandwiches
Michelle Moorman Caves

Desserts & Sweets
Dori Sponcler Jones

Main Dishes & Entrées
Heather Elwood Watley

Children's Cuisine & Confections
Mary Lynn Pugh Grubb

From Barstools to Bleachers

Appetizers & Beverages

Skipping school to go to Dinglewood Pharmacy for lunch is a Columbus tradition

and a tradition for my family as well. My grandparents, parents, and I all skipped school to

"pull up a stool" at the Dinglewood lunch counter!

This beloved Columbus establishment has been a mecca for medicines, conversations, and

especially scrumptious scrambled dogs for over eighty years.

—Robin Alexander Grier

From Barstools to Bleachers

Appetizers & Beverages

Salmon Mousse with Sour Cream Dill Sauce

Serves 14

Mousse	Sour Cream Dill Sauce
1 envelope unflavored gelatin	2 teaspoons dill weed
1/4 cup cold water	1 1/2 cups sour cream
1/2 cup boiling water	1 egg, beaten
1/2 cup mayonnaise	1 teaspoon salt
1 tablespoon grated onion	4 teaspoons lemon juice
1/2 teaspoon Tabasco sauce	1 teaspoon grated onion
2 tablespoons lemon juice	
1/4 teaspoon paprika	
1 teaspoon salt	
2 cups salmon, drained and finely chopped	
1 tablespoon capers, chopped	
1/2 cup heavy whipping cream	
3 cups cottage cheese (optional)	

To prepare the mousse, soften the gelatin in the cold water in a bowl. Add the boiling water and stir until dissolved. Let stand until cool. Add the mayonnaise, onion, Tabasco sauce, lemon juice, paprika and salt and mix well. Chill until the mousse is the consistency of unbeaten egg white. Add the salmon and capers and mix well. Whip the whipping cream in a mixing bowl until firm peaks form. Fold into the salmon mixture. Spoon into an oiled 2-quart fish mold. Add the cottage cheese to fill the mold. Chill until firm.

To prepare the sauce, combine the dill weed, sour cream, egg, salt, lemon juice and onion in a bowl and mix well.

To serve, unmold the mousse onto a serving platter. Pour the sauce over the mousse. Serve with crackers.

Note: If you are concerned about using raw eggs, use eggs pasteurized in their shells, which are sold at some specialty food stores, or use an equivalent amount of pasteurized egg substitute.

Catherine Zimmerman Bickerstaff

Baked Oysters Divine

Serves 6

1/4 cup (1/2 stick) butter	Worcestershire sauce to taste
3 garlic cloves, pressed	Salt to taste
3 slices white bread, toasted and crumbled	2 tablespoons chopped parsley
3 tablespoons grated Parmesan cheese, or to taste	1 1/2 pints oysters, drained (about 36)
Dash of Tabasco sauce	Rock salt
	Lemon juice

Melt the butter in a small saucepan. Stir in the garlic. Remove from the heat. Add the bread crumbs, cheese, Tabasco sauce, Worcestershire sauce, salt and parsley and mix well. Adjust the seasonings to taste. Place each drained oyster in an oyster shell or small ramekin and then in a large baking pan filled with rock salt. Squeeze lemon juice over each oyster and cover with the crumb mixture. Bake at 350 or 400 degrees for 15 to 20 minutes or until the oysters curl.

Note: The crumb mixture can be prepared and chilled the day before.

Ruth Combs Flowers

Shrimp Mousse

Serves 16

2 envelopes unflavored gelatin	3/4 cup finely chopped green onions
1/4 cup cold water	1 (4-ounce) can shrimp, drained and mashed
1 (10-ounce) can tomato soup	
16 ounces cream cheese, cut into cubes	1 tablespoon Worcestershire sauce
1 cup mayonnaise	3 tablespoons lemon juice
3/4 cup finely chopped celery	

Soften the gelatin in the cold water in a bowl. Bring the soup to a boil in a saucepan. Add the cream cheese and gelatin. Heat until smooth, stirring constantly. Remove from the heat to cool. Stir in the mayonnaise, celery, green onions, shrimp, Worcestershire sauce and lemon juice. Pour into a mold. Chill for several hours before serving. Unmold onto a serving platter and serve with your favorite crackers.

Note: The mousse can be stored in the refrigerator for several days.

Julie Hattaway Hinson

Ceviche

Serves 6

1 pound white fish, such as tilapia, sea bass or scallops
Juice of 2 limes
1 small onion, chopped
2 small tomatoes, chopped
2 tablespoons chopped jalapeño chiles

1 teaspoon chopped parsley
1 tablespoon capers
1/4 cup olive oil
1 to 2 tablespoons vinegar
Tabasco sauce to taste
Salt and pepper to taste

Chop the fish, discarding the skin and bones. Place in a shallow dish or glass pottery dish. Pour the lime juice over the fish. Marinate in the refrigerator for 3 hours or longer, turning with a wooden spoon until the fish flakes easily. Add the onion, tomatoes, jalapeño chiles, parsley, capers, olive oil, vinegar, Tabasco sauce, salt and pepper. Be generous with the seasonings to taste. Chill until serving time. Serve over shredded lettuce as a first course or with tortilla chips.

Fitzgerald Dunn Bickerstaff

Sautéed Crab Fingers

Serves 6 to 8

1 (16-ounce) container shelled crab fingers
3/4 cup (1 1/2 sticks) butter
1/4 teaspoon cayenne pepper or Cajun seasoning (optional)

2 teaspoons Greek seasoning
Juice of 2 lemons
Grated Parmesan cheese to taste

Rinse and drain the crab claws. Melt 1/4 cup of the butter in a large saucepan. Add the cayenne pepper, 1 teaspoon of the Greek seasoning and the juice of half a lemon. Heat over medium heat until the butter is bubbly. Add the crab claws. Sauté for 5 minutes. Cut the remaining butter into 1/4-inch slices and add to the crab claws. Cook until the butter is melted, stirring constantly. Sprinkle with the remaining 1 teaspoon Greek seasoning. Drizzle with the juice of half a lemon. Sauté for 2 to 4 minutes. Arrange the crab claws in a foil-lined medium baking pan. Sprinkle with cheese. Bake at 400 degrees for 5 to 7 minutes or until the cheese melts. Place in a serving dish and drizzle with the juice of the remaining lemon. Serve hot.

Note: Create your own seasoning with garlic powder, salt, black pepper and cayenne pepper. The garlic powder is the key. Cayenne pepper or Cajun seasoning should be added only if you enjoy the heat.

Laura Leggett Raines

Barbecue Shrimp New Orleans Style

Serves 10

2 cups (4 sticks) butter, melted
3 tablespoons Worcestershire sauce
2 tablespoons pepper

1 tablespoon garlic powder
1/2 teaspoon salt
5 pounds unpeeled deveined large shrimp

Mix the butter, Worcestershire sauce, pepper, garlic powder and salt in a bowl. Cook the shrimp in a Dutch oven over medium heat for 3 minutes or until the shrimp turn pink, stirring constantly. Remove from the heat. Stir in the butter mixture. Return to the heat and cook for 10 minutes, stirring constantly. Spoon into a serving dish. Keep covered until serving time.

Edie Pendleton Evans

Pickled Shrimp

Serves 20

Pickled shrimp has been a staple at many Columbus cocktail parties over the generations.

5 pounds shrimp, cooked, peeled and deveined
10 mild white onions, thinly sliced
10 celery tops with leaves
2 to 3 lemons, thinly sliced and seeded
2/3 pint cider vinegar
2 cups vegetable oil
1 (3-ounce) bottle capers

1 tablespoon sugar
1 teaspoon Worcestershire sauce
3 or 4 dashes of Tabasco sauce
1/2 teaspoon salt
2 to 3 tablespoons celery seeds
1 teaspoon pepper
3 garlic cloves

Place a layer of shrimp and a layer of onion slices in the bottom of a large jar or other container with a tight-fitting lid. Tuck the celery tops and lemon slices on the side. Repeat until the jar is full. Process the vinegar, oil, undrained capers, sugar, Worcestershire sauce, Tabasco sauce, salt, celery seeds, pepper and garlic in a blender until blended. Pour over the shrimp and seal the lid. Marinate in the refrigerator for 8 to 10 hours, turning the jar frequently.

Note: The shrimp can be stored in the refrigerator for 1 week.

Jean Dudley Illges

Sanny's Cheese Straws

Makes about 4 dozen

1 pound extra-sharp Cheddar cheese, at room temperature
3/4 cup (1 1/2 sticks) margarine, softened

1 to 1 1/2 teaspoons cayenne pepper
1 teaspoon salt
2 cups all-purpose flour

Shred the cheese into a large mixing bowl. Add the margarine, cayenne pepper and salt and mix well. Stir in the flour by hand. Spoon into a cookie press fitted with a small thin flat tip. Press onto an ungreased baking sheet. Bake at 350 degrees for 20 minutes or until firm but not brown, checking for doneness frequently. Remove from the oven to cool. Store in an airtight container.

Mary Lynn Pugh Grubb

Parmesan Puffs

Makes 12 to 18

These treats also make great accompaniments to soups and salads. Try other options for toppings on the bread, such as scallions, sun-dried tomatoes, sliced green olives, roasted garlic, or your own favorites.

2 shallots, chopped
Olive oil for sautéing
1 egg
1/2 cup milk
9 slices white bread

1 1/2 cups (6 ounces) grated Parmesan cheese
1/2 teaspoon cayenne pepper
1/2 cup (1 stick) butter, melted

Sauté the shallots in olive oil in a skillet over medium heat for 7 minutes. Beat the egg and milk in a medium bowl. Soak 1 slice of the bread in the milk mixture. Place on top of a dry slice of bread. Sprinkle with one-third of the sautéed shallots. Top with another slice of dry bread to create a sandwich with the soaked bread in the center. Repeat to form a total of three sandwiches. Press the top of each sandwich gently to make sure the bread slices stick together. Cut each sandwich into four or six pieces.

Mix the cheese and cayenne pepper in a small bowl. Dip each sandwich piece in the butter and then in the cheese mixture. Place on a baking sheet. Chill or freeze for 4 hours or longer. Bake at 350 degrees for 10 to 15 minutes or until very light brown, adding 5 minutes to the baking time if frozen.

Lee Helton Tyra

Parmesan Mushroom Squares

Serves 10 to 12

2 tablespoons butter
3 cups baby bella (button) mushrooms, drained well
2 tablespoons finely chopped onion
1/8 teaspoon garlic powder
1 teaspoon Worcestershire sauce

1 teaspoon lemon juice
1 (8-count) can refrigerator crescent rolls
3 ounces cream cheese, softened
1 1/2 cups (6 ounces) freshly grated Parmesan cheese

Melt the butter in a saucepan. Add the mushrooms, onion, garlic powder, Worcestershire sauce and lemon juice. Cook over medium-high heat for 10 minutes or until the liquid is reduced and the onion is translucent; drain well. Unroll the crescent roll dough on a baking sheet, pressing the perforations to seal. Spread a thin layer of cream cheese over the crescent roll dough. Spread the mushroom mixture over the cream cheese. Sprinkle with the Parmesan cheese. Bake at 375 degrees for 10 to 13 minutes or until the edges of the dough are golden brown. Cut into squares and serve warm.

Elizabeth Chambliss Gross

Stuffed Mushrooms

Makes 50

1 pound bulk Italian sausage
1/2 cup (2 ounces) shredded Parmesan cheese

8 ounces cream cheese
50 whole mushrooms

Brown the sausage in a skillet, stirring until crumbly; drain. Remove from the heat. Add the Parmesan cheese and cream cheese and mix well. Rinse the mushrooms and pat dry. Remove the stems from the mushrooms. Spoon the sausage mixture into the mushroom caps. Place in miniature muffin cups sprayed with nonstick cooking spray. Bake at 400 degrees for 10 minutes or until light brown.

Julie Davenport Davis

Sweet and Spicy Bacon

Serves 24

This is a guest favorite at our annual "Christmas Eve Eve" party, especially with the men.

12 slices thick-cut bacon
1/2 cup packed dark brown sugar
1/2 teaspoon cayenne pepper, or to taste
2 tablespoons water

Cut the bacon into halves. Combine the bacon, brown sugar, cayenne pepper and water in a bowl and mix well to coat. Line the bottom of a broiler pan with foil for easy cleanup. Spray the rack with nonstick cooking spray. Arrange the bacon side by side on the rack. Bake at 375 degrees for 15 minutes. Turn the bacon and bake for 10 minutes longer or until cooked through, watching carefully to prevent burning.

Note: The bacon can be prepared early and chilled until baking time.

Jeanie Hinson Bross

Magnolia's Spiced Pecans

Serves 12

6 tablespoons sugar
1/4 cup (1/2 stick) butter, melted
1/4 cup Worcestershire sauce
2 teaspoons cayenne pepper
2 teaspoons Creole seasoning
1 tablespoon granulated garlic or garlic powder
1 teaspoon salt
1/2 teaspoon black pepper
1 pound pecan halves

Combine the sugar, butter, Worcestershire sauce, cayenne pepper, Creole seasoning, garlic, salt and black pepper in a bowl and mix well. Add the pecans and toss until coated. Spread on a baking sheet. Bake at 275 degrees for 25 to 30 minutes or until brown. Use as an hors d'oeuvre or sprinkle on top of salads.

Elvis (Kip) Hammersley, Jr.

Marinated Vegetables

Serves 12 to 14

1 tablespoon (or less) sugar
1 tablespoon dill weed
2 teaspoons (or more) Accent (optional)
1 teaspoon salt
1 teaspoon pepper
1 teaspoon garlic powder
1 cup cider vinegar
1 cup vegetable oil
1 (15-ounce) can green peas, drained
1 (15-ounce) can lima beans, drained
1 (11-ounce) can Shoe Peg corn, drained

2 (14-ounce) cans French-style green
   beans, drained
1 (8-ounce) can water chestnuts,
   drained and sliced (optional)
1 (4-ounce) can pimentos,
   drained and sliced
1 green bell pepper, chopped
1 cup chopped celery
2 bunches green onions, chopped
Melba toast rounds

Mix the sugar, dill weed, Accent, salt, pepper, garlic powder, vinegar and oil in a bowl. Combine the green peas, lima beans, corn, green beans, water chestnuts, pimentos, bell pepper, celery and green onions in a bowl and mix well. Add the marinade and mix well. Marinate, covered, in the refrigerator for 24 hours. Spoon onto melba toast rounds to serve.

Note: This may also be served as a cool side dish with a sandwich on a hot summer day.

Carolyn Zollo Crenshaw, Spartanburg, South Carolina

*L*earning, talking, and enjoying good food always occurred while sitting on stools at the island in our kitchen. Whether it was junior high school girls gossiping and snacking, high school girls talking about prom dresses, or my future husband and I celebrating our engagement with Champagne, I never realized the roles those stools played in bringing together so many people that I love.

— *Mary Lynn Pugh Grubb*

Spinach Phyllo

Makes 3 dozen

5 sheets phyllo dough
1 (12-ounce) package frozen spinach soufflé
1 tablespoon lemon juice
1/4 teaspoon salt
1/4 teaspoon cayenne pepper
1 (8-ounce) package feta cheese, crumbled
Cayenne pepper for garnish

Lay 1 sheet of the phyllo dough on a work surface and spray lightly with olive oil nonstick cooking spray, keeping the remaining phyllo sheets covered with plastic wrap to prevent drying out. Top with another sheet of the phyllo dough and spray with nonstick cooking spray. Repeat three times with the remaining phyllo dough. Cut the phyllo stack into 6-inch squares. Fit each square into a muffin cup. Bake at 350 degrees for 10 minutes. Maintain the oven temperature.

Cook the spinach soufflé using the package directions. Stir in the lemon juice, salt and 1/4 teaspoon cayenne pepper. Divide evenly among the baked phyllo cups. Sprinkle the cheese on top. Garnish with cayenne pepper. Bake for 6 minutes.

Lisa McMullen Allen

Olive Cheese Balls

Serves 20

This recipe was contributed by Sandra Rodgers, a much sought-after private caterer in Columbus, Georgia.

48 small pimento-stuffed olives
8 ounces sharp Cheddar cheese, shredded
1 1/4 cups all-purpose flour
1/2 cup (1 stick) butter, melted

Drain the olives and place on paper towels to dry. Mix the cheese and flour in a bowl until crumbly. Add the butter and mix to form a ball. Pinch off a small piece of the dough and flatten on the palm of your hand. Place a dry olive on the flattened dough and wrap around the olive to form a ball. Place on a baking sheet. Repeat with the remaining dough and olives. Chill, covered, for 1 hour. Bake at 400 degrees for 15 to 20 minutes.

Note: Do not use pre-shredded cheese in this recipe. The olives must be completely dry before wrapping with the dough.

Sandra Rodgers

Buffalo Chicken Dip

Serves 12

Great for tailgating.

5 or 6 boneless skinless chicken breasts, cooked and finely chopped
5 ounces hot pepper sauce
16 ounces cream cheese, softened
1 cup blue cheese salad dressing
2 cups (8 ounces) shredded Monterey Jack cheese

Toss the chicken with the hot sauce in a bowl and place in a baking dish. Beat the cream cheese and salad dressing in a bowl until smooth. Spread over the chicken. Sprinkle with the Monterey Jack cheese. Bake at 350 degrees for 30 minutes. Serve with corn chip scoops.

Whitney Rice Pease

Black Bean and Feta Dip

Serves 8 to 10

2 (14-ounce) cans Shoe Peg corn, drained
2 (15-ounce) cans black beans, drained
4 or 5 scallions, sliced
8 ounces feta cheese, crumbled
1/2 cup sugar
3/4 cup vegetable oil
3/4 cup apple cider vinegar
1/2 teaspoon garlic salt, or to taste

Combine the corn, beans, scallions and cheese in a bowl. Mix the sugar, oil, vinegar and garlic salt in a bowl. Pour over the corn mixture and mix well. Serve with tortilla chips or corn chip scoops.

Sarah Linne Sluder

Fiesta Corn Dip

Serves 10 to 12

2 (10-ounce) cans Mexicorn
3 (10-ounce) cans tomatoes with green chiles, drained
1 (4-ounce) can green chiles, drained
3 cups (12 ounces) shredded Cheddar cheese
1 cup sour cream
1 cup mayonnaise
Seasoning salt to taste

Combine the Mexicorn, tomatoes with green chiles, green chiles, cheese, sour cream, mayonnaise and seasoning salt in a bowl and mix well. Chill, covered, for 2 hours. Stir well before serving. Serve with tortilla chips or corn chips.

Sarah Linne Sluder

Curry Dip for Raw Vegetables

Serves 12

2 cups mayonnaise
1/2 cup sour cream
1/8 teaspoon turmeric
2 tablespoons curry powder
2 garlic cloves, minced, or 11/2 teaspoons garlic powder
4 teaspoons sugar
2 teaspoons salt
2 teaspoons lemon juice
1/4 cup parsley, minced

Mix the mayonnaise, sour cream, turmeric, curry powder, garlic, sugar, salt, lemon juice and parsley in a bowl. Chill, covered, for 8 to 10 hours before serving. Serve as a dip with cauliflower florets, carrots, celery, yellow squash sticks and asparagus.

Note: Make sure the vegetables are crisp by icing them down ahead of time.

Cornelia Stokes Bussey

Fresh Guacamole Dip

Serves 4 to 6

4 ripe Haas avocados, cut into chunks
Juice of 1 lemon
1 garlic clove, minced
1/2 (or less) small red onion, chopped
8 dashes of Tabasco sauce
1 teaspoon salt
1 teaspoon pepper
1 tomato, seeded and chopped

Combine the avocados, lemon juice, garlic, onion, Tabasco sauce, salt and pepper in a bowl and toss to mix. Stir in the tomato. Do not overmix.

Kathy Ann Martin

Jamie's Totally Awesome Salsa

Serves 12

*Jamie is a talented friend of the Junior League of Columbus.
He has directed our last three Follies, which are musical and dance revues
starring league members. We have raised nearly half a million dollars to
support the community through these productions.*

1 (28-ounce) can diced tomatoes, drained, or 8 large tomatoes, chopped
1 (6-ounce) can tomato paste
2 (4-ounce) cans chopped green chiles
1/3 cup olive oil
1/3 cup apple cider vinegar
1/3 cup hot pepper sauce, or to taste
1 teaspoon pepper

Combine the tomatoes and tomato paste in a medium bowl and mix well. Stir in the green chiles, olive oil, vinegar, hot sauce and pepper. Chill, covered, until serving time. Serve with tortilla chips.

Jamie Donegan, Philadelphia, Pennsylvania

Good Times Tex-Mex Dip

Serves 12 to 14

8 ounces cream cheese, softened
2 cups sour cream
1 envelope taco seasoning mix
1 (10-ounce) can mild tomatoes with green chiles, drained
1 (10-ounce) can hot tomatoes with green chiles, drained
1 pound sharp Cheddar cheese, shredded
1 (3-ounce) can sliced black olives

Combine the cream cheese, sour cream and taco seasoning mix in a bowl and mix until smooth. Spread in a 9×13-inch glass dish. Spread the mild and hot tomatoes with green chiles evenly over the cream cheese layer. Sprinkle with the Cheddar cheese. Top with the olives. Serve with tortilla chips or corn chip scoops.

Millie Peacock Patrick

Elegant Spinach and Artichoke Spread

Serves 20

This is a hearty and delicious spread to serve, especially when entertaining during the fall and winter months.

1 cup finely chopped onion
5 garlic cloves, minced
3 tablespoons butter
4 cups chopped fresh spinach
1 (14-ounce) can chopped artichoke hearts
8 ounces cream cheese, softened
1 cup (4 ounces) shredded Parmesan cheese
1 cup (4 ounces) shredded Cheddar cheese

1 cup (4 ounces) shredded Monterey Jack cheese
1/2 cup mayonnaise
2 pinches of salt
3/4 cup chopped pecans
1/2 cup Italian bread crumbs
1 tablespoon butter, melted
Few thin pats of butter for topping

Sauté the onion and garlic in 3 tablespoons butter in a skillet until soft. Add the spinach and sauté for 3 to 4 minutes or until the spinach wilts. Add the artichokes, cream cheese, Parmesan cheese, Cheddar cheese, Monterey Jack cheese and mayonnaise. Heat until the cheese melts, stirring constantly. Spoon into a greased 1 1/2-quart baking dish. Sprinkle with the salt. Bake at 350 degrees for 25 minutes. Mix the pecans, bread crumbs and 1 tablespoon butter in a bowl. Stir the hot cheese mixture and top with the pecan mixture. Place a few thin pats of butter over the top to moisten. Bake for 20 minutes. Serve with pita chips, corn chip scoops or your favorite chips.

Edie Pendleton Evans

"Pull up a chair" is typically an invitation to join others in a group.

Blue Cheese Ball

Serves 10 to 12

11 ounces cream cheese, softened
1/2 cup (1 stick) butter, softened
4 ounces blue cheese
1 (4-ounce) can black olives, drained and chopped
1 small Vidalia onion, chopped
Finely chopped pecans for rolling

Place the cream cheese, butter, blue cheese, olives and onion in a bowl. Let stand for 30 minutes to soften and then mix together. Shape into a ball and roll in pecans. Serve with thin wheat crackers or your favorite crackers.

Allison Weaver Peak

Holiday Cheese Ring

Serves 8 to 10

1 pound sharp Cheddar cheese, shredded
1/2 cup chopped green onions
1 cup mayonnaise
1 cup pecans, chopped
Cayenne pepper to taste
5 to 6 tablespoons strawberry preserves or jam

Combine the cheese, green onions, mayonnaise, pecans and cayenne pepper in a bowl and mix well. Place in a ring mold or other desired container. Chill in the refrigerator. Unmold onto a serving platter and top with the strawberry preserves. Serve with crackers or melba toast rounds.

Shirley Monacelli Kurtz Craddock

Festive Pesto Spread

Serves 12 to 14

16 ounces cream cheese, softened
2 envelopes zesty Italian salad dressing mix
1/2 cup pine nuts
1/2 cup drained pesto
1 (14-ounce) can chopped petite diced tomatoes, drained
Salt and pepper to taste
Seasoned salt to taste
Sprig of fresh rosemary for garnish

Combine the cream cheese, salad dressing mix and pine nuts in a bowl and mix well. Line a small container with plastic wrap. Layer the pesto then the cream cheese mixture in the prepared container. Chill for several hours. Mix the tomatoes, salt, pepper and seasoned salt in a bowl. Drain any excess liquid from the tomatoes. Reserve a few diced tomatoes for garnish. Place the remaining tomatoes on a serving plate. Invert the spread onto the tomatoes and remove the plastic wrap. Garnish with the reserved tomatoes and rosemary. Serve with crackers or toast.

Susan Cheney Gilliam

Blue Moon Pimento Cheese

Makes about 3 cups

2 cups (8 ounces) shredded sharp Cheddar cheese
1/2 cup good-quality chili sauce
3/4 cup mayonnaise
1/2 cup pimento-stuffed green olives, chopped
1/2 cup chopped pecans
1 teaspoon Worcestershire sauce
1/2 teaspoon seasoned salt
Garlic salt to taste

Mix the cheese, chili sauce, mayonnaise, olives, pecans, Worcestershire sauce, seasoned salt and garlic salt in a bowl. Place in a serving bowl. Serve on crackers or pita toast.

Cora Copelan Lee, Dothan, Alabama

Lake Martin Smoothie

Serves 4 or 5

The rum may be omitted for a tasty drink fitting for all ages.

1 (6-ounce) can frozen limeade concentrate or pink lemonade concentrate
4 or 5 peaches, chopped
4 to 5 tablespoons chopped peach skin for color and flavor
1 cup white rum, or to taste
1/2 to 1 banana
Ice

Place the limeade concentrate, peaches, peach skin, rum and banana in a blender container. Fill completely with ice. Process until smooth. Pour into serving glasses.

Note: Strawberries can be added, too.

Donna Sears Hand

Steve's Special Bloody Mary

Serves 6

*This recipe was perfected by Steve Kurowsky, who was
a chemist at Callaway Chemical. He worked regularly on this recipe
to make sure the ingredients were just right.*

1 (64-ounce) bottle clamato juice
2 cups vodka
3/4 tablespoon celery salt
3/4 tablespoon lemon pepper
2 tablespoons Worcestershire sauce
2 teaspoons Tabasco sauce
1 tablespoon lime juice
3 tablespoons horseradish

Combine the clamato juice, vodka, celery salt, lemon pepper, Worcestershire sauce, Tabasco sauce, lime juice and horseradish in a pitcher and mix well. Pour into glasses.

Robin Alexander Grier

Fresh Margaritas

Serves 6

Best served outside with good friends.

4 ounces fresh lime juice
Juice of 1/2 lemon
2 tablespoons sugar
1 cup Triple Sec
4 cups ice
1 cup tequila
6 splashes of Grand Marnier

Process the lime juice, lemon juice, sugar, Triple Sec, ice and tequila in a blender until blended. Pour into salt-rimmed margarita glasses and add a splash of Grand Marnier.

Kathy Ann Martin

Citrus Mimosas

Serves 8

1 cup prepared strawberry daiquiri mix
1 (6-ounce) can frozen orange juice concentrate, thawed
3/4 cup water
1/3 cup fresh grapefruit juice
1/2 (6-ounce) can frozen lemonade concentrate, thawed
3 tablespoons frozen limeade concentrate, thawed
1 (750-milliliter) bottle Champagne, chilled
8 thin orange slices, cut into halves

Combine the daiquiri mix, orange juice concentrate, water, grapefruit juice, lemonade concentrate, limeade concentrate, Champagne and orange slice halves in a pitcher and mix well. Pour into Champagne glasses.

Cammy Diaz Marchetti

E. V.'s Derby Day Mint Julep

Serves 6

1 cup sugar
1 cup hot water
2 tablespoons mint leaves (about 2 to 3 sprigs of mint)
9 ounces good-quality bourbon
2 cups crushed ice, or to taste
Sprigs of fresh mint for garnish

Prepare the mint syrup in advance. Dissolve the sugar in the hot water in a small pitcher. Add the mint leaves and let stand for several hours. For each serving, place 2 1/2 teaspoons of the mint syrup and 1 1/2 ounces of the bourbon in a silver julep cup and fill with the ice. Garnish with a sprig of mint. Store the remaining mint syrup in the refrigerator.

William Lanier (Putt) Church

Baby Punch

Makes 2 quarts

This is an excellent drink to serve at a brunch or baby shower. Be sure to prepare this in advance to allow time for freezing.

1 family-size tea bag, or 3 regular-size tea bags
1 cup boiling water
1 (6-ounce) can frozen orange juice concentrate
1 (6-ounce) can frozen lemonade concentrate
3 1/2 cups water
1/2 cup sugar
1 cup amaretto
1 (2-liter) bottle diet ginger ale or regular ginger ale

Steep the tea bag in 1 cup boiling water. Combine the orange juice concentrate, lemonade concentrate, 3 1/2 cups water, the sugar and amaretto in a freezer container and mix well. Add the tea and mix well. Freeze until firm. Place in a punch bowl and add the ginger ale. Ladle into punch cups.

Dori Sponcler Jones

Cranberry Vodka Punch

Serves 10 to 12

1 (16-ounce) bottle cranberry juice cocktail
8 ounces vodka
2 ounces lime juice
8 ounces ginger ale
4 teaspoons sugar
Ice ring

Combine the cranberry juice cocktail, vodka, lime juice, ginger ale and sugar in a container and mix well. Pour into a punch bowl and add an ice ring. Ladle into punch cups.

Note: You may also serve over ice.

Hilda Hughes Church, Dothan, Alabama

Milk Punch

Serves 4

1 gallon vanilla ice cream
6 ounces brandy
2 ounces white crème de cacao
2 cups ice
1/8 teaspoon nutmeg

Fill a blender container three-fourths full with the ice cream. Add the brandy and crème de cacao. Add enough ice to fill the container. Process until blended. Pour into glasses and sprinkle with the nutmeg.

Jane Bullock Wiley

Banana Punch

Serves 10 to 12

2 cups sugar
3 cups water
1 quart pineapple juice
1 (6-ounce) can frozen orange juice concentrate
Juice of 1 lemon
2 or 3 bananas, puréed
2 drops of yellow food coloring (optional)
1 (2-liter) bottle (or more) ginger ale

Simmer the sugar and water in a saucepan over medium-high heat until the sugar is dissolved, stirring constantly. Let cool to room temperature. Combine with the pineapple juice, orange juice concentrate, lemon juice, banana purée and food coloring in a pitcher and mix well. Pour into an attractive mold. Freeze until firm.

To serve, unmold the frozen mixture into a punch bowl. Cover with ginger ale. Continue to add the remaining ginger ale as needed. The frozen mixture will keep the punch cool and will slowly melt.

Note: Using three bananas yields a strong banana taste. For a less intense banana flavor, use two bananas.

Edith Harwell McCullough

Iced Tea Fizz

Serves 6 to 8

4 green tea bags or your favorite tea
2 cups boiling water
1 (12-ounce) can frozen cranberry-raspberry juice concentrate
1/2 gallon club soda, chilled
Ice
12 to 16 fresh raspberries for garnish
6 to 8 sprigs of fresh mint for garnish

Steep the tea bags in the boiling water in a pitcher. Discard the tea bags and stir in the cranberry-raspberry concentrate. Chill until serving time. To serve, fill glasses one-fourth full with the tea. Add club soda and ice. Garnish each serving with 2 fresh raspberries and a sprig of mint.

Anne Hayes Drinkard Pearce

Spiced Tea

Serves 22

1 (18-ounce) jar orange drink mix
1/2 cup sugar
1 teaspoon cinnamon
1 teaspoon ground cloves
3/4 cup instant tea granules with sugar and lemon

Mix the drink mix, sugar, cinnamon, cloves and tea granules in a bowl. Store in an airtight container. For each serving, dissolve 2 teaspoons of the spiced tea mix in 1 cup boiling water.

Elaine Tribble McMillen

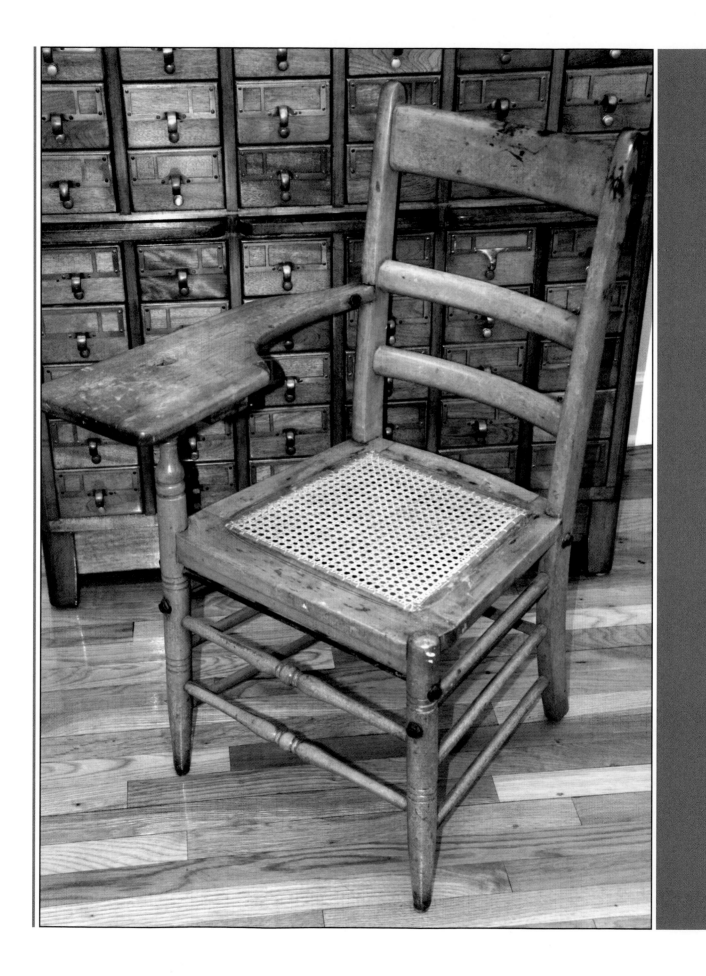

From Bentwoods to Booths

Breakfast & Breads

Volunteering as a Room Reader at Wynnton School, our Partner in Education,

was a rewarding experience for me. The children and I developed friendships. They hugged me,

laughed with me, shared exciting news with me, and even invited me to attend other school events.

Each week when I arrived, my "special" chair would be ready—placed strategically in the middle

of the carpeted area in the classroom. Most days I would sit in a regular-size chair, like the teacher's.

Sometimes I'd be lucky enough to sit in a much smaller, student-size chair!

Our league has provided significant assistance for special projects,

school room readers, and supplies for decades.

—Kelly Flournoy Pridgen

From Bentwoods to Booths

Breakfast & Breads

Scrambled Eggs in Pumpernickel Toast Cups

Serves 4

4 slices pumpernickel bread
2 tablespoons butter, softened
10 eggs
1 teaspoon coarse salt
1/4 teaspoon pepper
1 cup (4 ounces) shredded Monterey Jack cheese
2 tablespoons olive oil
4 pinches of freshly chopped chives

Spread both sides of the bread with the butter. Press the bread firmly into four jumbo muffin cups. Bake at 400 degrees for 15 to 20 minutes or until crisp.

Whisk the eggs, salt and pepper in a large bowl. Whisk in the cheese. Heat the olive oil in a nonstick skillet over medium-high heat. Add the egg mixture. Cook for 8 to 10 minutes or until set, stirring frequently.

Remove the toast cups from the muffin cups and place on serving plates. Spoon the scrambled eggs into the toast cups and sprinkle with the chives.

Hadley Upchurch Scott

"*As nervous as a long-tailed cat in a room full of rocking chairs*" means one is very anxious.

Cream Cheese Eggs

Serves 6

6 tablespoons butter
12 eggs
4 ounces cream cheese, softened
1 cup half-and-half
3/4 teaspoon salt
1/4 teaspoon pepper
1/4 cup chopped fresh parsley

Melt the butter in a skillet over low heat. Process the eggs, cream cheese, half-and-half, salt and pepper at medium speed in a blender for 7 to 10 seconds or until smooth. Pour into the butter. Cook over low heat until the eggs are set but still moist, stirring frequently. Sprinkle with the parsley.

Shannan Hartley Bickerstaff

Baked Omelet

Serves 4 to 6

8 eggs
1/2 cup sour cream
1 1/2 teaspoons salt
1 cup (4 ounces) shredded cheese
1 teaspoon butter, melted

Beat the eggs, sour cream and salt in a bowl until blended. Stir in the cheese. Pour into a buttered 1/2-quart loaf pan and drizzle with the butter. Bake at 350 degrees for 30 minutes or until puffed and set.

Whitney Rice Pease

Easy Eggs Benedict

Serves 6

This recipe is easily doubled without much extra time and effort.

Hollandaise Sauce	Eggs Benedict
4 egg yolks	3 English muffins, split
1/2 teaspoon salt	6 eggs
1/2 teaspoon dry mustard	6 slices Canadian bacon
1 tablespoon lemon juice	
Dash of Tabasco sauce, or to taste	
1/2 cup (1 stick) butter, melted	

To prepare the sauce, blend the egg yolks, salt, dry mustard, lemon juice and Tabasco sauce in a blender. Add the butter in a steady stream, processing constantly until blended. Heat in a double boiler over hot water just until warm. Do not heat until hot or the sauce will harden.

To prepare the eggs Benedict, toast the English muffins and keep warm. Crack the eggs into greased muffin cups. Bake at 350 degrees for 10 to 12 minutes or to the desired degree of doneness. Cook the Canadian bacon in a skillet over medium heat until heated through. Layer an English muffin, a slice of Canadian bacon and an egg on each serving plate. Serve with the sauce.

Shannan Hartley Bickerstaff

My brother and I often roused my mother from her sleep on Saturdays far earlier than she would have preferred. She would drag herself out of bed very begrudgingly to make her way to the coffeepot. To make us feel special, my mom would take out my great-grandmother's tea set and fill the demitasses (mostly with milk for us) with that first cup of Joe. She allowed us to savor that moment with her. We would sit at the dining room table to have our morning coffee. The chairs were so big and I was so small. We felt so privileged to share in that time with her.

— Resa Pate Carter

Salsa Omelet

Serves 4

3/4 cup (or more) salsa	8 eggs, beaten
1 cup (4 ounces) shredded Monterey Jack cheese	1/2 cup sour cream
1 cup (4 ounces) shredded Cheddar cheese	1/2 cup cottage cheese
	Salt and pepper to taste

Spread the salsa in a greased 9-inch deep-dish pie plate. Layer the Monterey Jack cheese and Cheddar cheese over the salsa. Mix the eggs, sour cream, cottage cheese, salt and pepper in a bowl. Pour over the cheese. Bake at 350 degrees for 45 to 55 minutes or until brown and set.

Crawford Pate Knox

Cheesy Brunch Pie

Serves 8

Prepare the parsley and bacon the night before to speed up the prep time...then throw it all together the next morning.

8 ounces bacon	2 tablespoons chopped fresh parsley
4 eggs	1 unbaked (10-inch) deep-dish pie shell
1 cup sour cream	Fresh parsley for garnish
8 ounces Swiss cheese, shredded	

Cook the bacon in a skillet until crisp. Remove to paper towels to drain. Crumble the bacon. Whisk the eggs and sour cream in a bowl until blended. Stir in the crumbled bacon, cheese and 2 tablespoons parsley. Pour into the pie shell and place on a baking sheet. Bake at 375 degrees for 40 to 50 minutes or until a knife inserted in the center comes out clean. Let stand for 15 minutes before serving. Garnish with fresh parsley.

Note: If you are unable to find a deep-dish pie shell, a 9-inch pie shell can be used.

Jessica DeLuca Hart

Quiche à la Crab

Serves 6

1/4 cup mushrooms	Dash of cayenne pepper
3 tablespoons butter	2 tablespoons vermouth or white wine
2 tablespoons chopped green onions	3 eggs
3 tablespoons chopped red bell pepper	1 cup half-and-half
1 cup crab meat, well drained	1 unbaked (9-inch) deep-dish pie shell
1/2 teaspoon salt, or to taste	1/2 cup (2 ounces) shredded Swiss cheese
1/2 teaspoon black pepper	Fresh parsley for garnish

Sauté the mushrooms in the butter in a skillet over medium heat for 5 minutes. Add the green onions and bell pepper. Simmer until soft. Add the crab meat, salt, black pepper and cayenne pepper. Add the wine. Cook for 1 minute. Remove from the heat to cool.

Beat the eggs lightly in a medium bowl. Whisk in the half-and-half. Add the crab meat mixture and mix well. Pour into the pie shell. Sprinkle with the cheese. Bake at 350 degrees for 25 minutes or until golden brown. Garnish with fresh parsley.

Gardiner Zollo Church

Leek and Tomato Quiche

Serves 6

1 leek
3 tablespoons unsalted butter
1 tablespoon olive oil
1 tablespoon all-purpose flour
4 eggs
1 1/3 cups half-and-half
6 ounces Swiss cheese, shredded
1 1/2 teaspoons salt
Freshly ground pepper
1 unbaked (10-inch) deep-dish pie shell
1 tomato, sliced
1 teaspoon dried oregano or Italian seasoning
2 tablespoons parsley leaves

Rinse the leek thoroughly and cut into slices. Melt the butter with the olive oil in a 9-inch skillet. Add the leek and sauté lightly. Stir in the flour and heat until warm. Do not cook. Remove from the heat.

Beat the eggs and half-and-half lightly in a bowl. Add the leek mixture, cheese, salt and pepper. Pour into the pie shell, discarding any excess filling. Arrange the tomato slices over the top. Sprinkle with the oregano and parsley. Bake at 375 degrees for 55 minutes or until brown and set. Let stand for 15 minutes before serving. Serve hot or at room temperature.

Note: Gruyère cheese can be used for one-half of the Swiss cheese.

Sally Bickerstaff Hatcher

Holiday Breakfast Casserole

Serves 10 to 12

8 slices white bread, crusts trimmed
9 eggs
3 cups milk
2 teaspoons dry mustard
1 teaspoon salt

2 pounds bulk pork sausage,
  cooked and crumbled
2 cups (8 ounces) shredded
  Cheddar cheese

Place the bread in a greased 9×13-inch baking dish. Beat the eggs, milk, dry mustard and salt in a bowl until blended. Add the sausage and cheese and mix well. Pour over the bread. Chill, covered, for 8 to 10 hours. Remove from the refrigerator and let stand at room temperature for 30 minutes before baking. Bake at 350 degrees for 45 to 60 minutes or until set.

Susan Carroll Schlader

Sausage and Cream Cheese Casserole

Serves 6 to 8

2 (8-count) cans refrigerator crescent rolls
1 pound bulk sausage
8 ounces cream cheese, melted
1 cup (4 ounces) shredded
  mozzarella cheese

1 cup (4 ounces) shredded
  Cheddar cheese
1 cup (4 ounces) shredded Colby
  Jack cheese

Unroll one can of the crescent roll dough. Place in a 9×13-inch baking dish, pressing the perforations to seal. Brown the sausage in a skillet, stirring until crumbly; drain. Add the cream cheese and mix well. Spread over the crescent roll dough. Sprinkle with the mozzarella cheese, Cheddar cheese and Colby Jack cheese. Unroll the remaining can of crescent roll dough and press the perforations to seal. Place over the top of the casserole, covering the cheese. Bake using the crescent roll can directions.

Robin Alexander Grier

Tahoe Brunch

Serves 8

2 to 3 tablespoons butter, softened	5 eggs
12 slices white bread, crusts trimmed	2¹/2 cups milk
¹/2 cup (1 stick) butter	1 teaspoon dry mustard
8 ounces mushrooms, sliced	1 tablespoon Dijon mustard
2 cups thinly sliced yellow onions	1 teaspoon nutmeg
Salt and pepper to taste	1 teaspoon salt
1¹/2 pounds Italian sausage	¹/2 teaspoon pepper
12 ounces Cheddar cheese, shredded	2 tablespoons chopped parsley

Spread 2 to 3 tablespoons butter on the bread. Melt ¹/2 cup butter in a skillet. Add the mushrooms and onions and sauté until brown. Add salt and pepper to taste. Cook the sausage in a skillet until cooked through. Cut into bite-size pieces. Layer the bread, sautéed vegetables, sausage and cheese one-half at a time in a greased 7×11-inch baking dish. Beat the eggs, milk, dry mustard, Dijon mustard, nutmeg, 1 teaspoon salt and ¹/2 teaspoon pepper in a bowl. Pour over the layers. Chill, covered, for 8 to 10 hours. Uncover and sprinkle with the parsley. Bake at 350 degrees for 1 hour or until bubbly.

Dori Sponcler Jones

Hash Brown Casserole

Serves 8 to 10

1 (32-ounce) package frozen hash brown potatoes	1 cup sour cream
¹/2 cup (1 stick) butter or margarine, melted	2¹/2 cups (10 ounces) finely shredded Cheddar cheese
1 teaspoon salt	3 cups crushed cornflakes
¹/4 teaspoon pepper	¹/4 cup (¹/2 stick) butter or margarine, melted
1¹/2 (10-ounce) cans cream of chicken soup	

Thaw the potatoes in the refrigerator for 8 to 10 hours or in the microwave. Place in a large bowl. Mix ¹/2 cup butter, the salt and pepper in a bowl. Add to the potatoes and mix well. Combine the soup, sour cream and cheese in a bowl and mix well. Add to the potato mixture and stir until evenly coated. Spoon into a greased 9×13-inch baking dish. Mix the cornflakes with ¹/4 cup butter in a bowl. Sprinkle over the top. Bake at 350 degrees for 45 minutes.

Colleen Day Rustin

Christmas Grits

Serves 10 to 12

1 cup uncooked grits	2 eggs
1 teaspoon salt	Milk
4 cups water	1 cup (4 ounces) shredded
1/2 cup (1 stick) butter	Cheddar cheese
5 ounces garlic and herb cheese	

Cook the grits with the salt in the water in a saucepan until thickened, stirring frequently. Melt the butter and garlic and herb cheese in a saucepan, stirring frequently. Add to the grits and mix well. Beat the eggs in a measuring cup. Add enough milk to measure 1 cup. Add to the grits mixture and mix well. Pour into a greased 2-quart baking dish. Sprinkle with the Cheddar cheese. Bake at 350 degrees for 25 minutes.

Dori Sponcler Jones

Gourmet Cheese Grits

Serves 8

1 quart milk	1 egg
1/2 cup (1 stick) butter	1/3 cup butter
1 cup uncooked grits	4 ounces Gruyère cheese, shredded
1 teaspoon salt	1/2 cup (2 ounces) freshly grated
Pepper to taste	Parmesan cheese

Bring the milk to a boil in a saucepan over medium heat, stirring frequently. Add 1/2 cup butter and the grits. Cook for 5 minutes or until the mixture is the consistency of oatmeal, stirring constantly. Remove from the heat. Add the salt, pepper and egg and beat well. Add 1/3 cup butter and the Gruyère cheese and mix until smooth. Pour into a greased 2-quart baking dish. Sprinkle with the Parmesan cheese. Bake at 350 degrees for 1 hour, covering with foil if the Parmesan cheese begins to brown.

Martha Gilliam Hatcher

European Oatmeal

Serves 6 to 8

This recipe is not intended to be cooked, but rather enjoyed at room temperature or warmed slightly.

4 cups rolled oats	1 cup walnuts, chopped
1 cup skim milk	1/3 cup raisins
1 cup half-and-half	1/3 cup dried cranberries
1 teaspoon cinnamon	1 Granny Smith apple, chopped
1/2 teaspoon nutmeg	1 red apple, chopped
3/4 cup packed brown sugar	Fresh seasonal berries for topping

Soak the oats in the milk and half-and-half in a large bowl until the liquid is absorbed. Stir in the cinnamon, nutmeg, brown sugar, walnuts, raisins and cranberries. Let stand for 20 to 30 minutes. Add the Granny Smith apple and red apple and mix well. Spoon into serving bowls and top with fresh seasonal berries.

Dori Sponcler Jones

Overnight Pecan French Toast

Serves 4

1/2 cup packed brown sugar	4 eggs
1/4 cup (1/2 stick) butter, cut into cubes	1 1/3 cups milk
2 tablespoons corn syrup	1 teaspoon vanilla extract
1/2 cup chopped pecans	1/4 teaspoon salt
8 (1-inch-thick) slices French bread	

Combine the brown sugar, butter and corn syrup in a small saucepan and mix well. Cook over medium heat for 3 minutes or until thickened, stirring constantly. Do not overcook. Pour into a greased 9×13-inch baking dish. Sprinkle with the pecans. Top with the bread. Whisk the eggs, milk, vanilla and salt in a bowl. Pour evenly over the bread. Chill, covered, for 8 to 10 hours.

Remove from the refrigerator and let stand at room temperature for 30 minutes before baking. Bake at 350 degrees for 35 to 40 minutes or until set. Invert onto a serving platter.

Charlene Roberts Marx

French Toast Strata with Apple Syrup

Serves 12

Strata	Apple Syrup
1 (1-pound) loaf unsliced French bread	1/2 cup sugar
8 ounces cream cheese, cut into cubes	4 teaspoons cornstarch
8 eggs	1/2 teaspoon cinnamon
2 1/2 cups half-and-half or milk	1 cup apple cider or apple juice
6 tablespoons butter, melted	1 tablespoon lemon juice
1/4 cup maple syrup	2 tablespoons butter

To prepare the strata, cut the bread into cubes. Place one-half of the bread in a greased 9×13-inch baking dish. Scatter the cream cheese cubes over the bread. Top with the remaining bread cubes. Process the eggs, half-and-half, butter and maple syrup in a blender until blended or beat in a mixing bowl. Pour over the layers, pressing with a spatula lightly to moisten. Chill, covered with plastic wrap, for 2 to 12 hours. Remove the plastic wrap. Bake at 325 degrees for 40 minutes or until the center appears set and the edges are light golden brown. Let stand for 10 minutes before serving.

To prepare the syrup, mix the sugar, cornstarch and cinnamon in a small saucepan. Stir in the apple cider and lemon juice. Cook over medium heat until thick and bubbly, stirring constantly. Remove from the heat. Stir in the butter.

To serve, cut the strata into squares and serve with the syrup.

Kay Stewart Berard

French Toast Kabobs

Serves 4

1 (1-pound) loaf unsliced white bread, crusts trimmed	1/4 teaspoon vanilla extract
	1/4 cup (1/2 stick) unsalted butter
8 eggs	2 bananas, sliced
2/3 cup reduced-fat buttermilk	1 cup blueberries
Pinch of salt	1 cup raspberries

Heat a rimmed baking sheet in a 250-degree oven. Cut the bread into 1-inch cubes. Whisk the eggs, buttermilk, salt and vanilla in a large bowl. Stir in the bread cubes until coated. Melt half the butter in a large skillet over medium heat. Add one-half of the bread cubes and cook until brown. Remove to the warm baking sheet in the oven to keep warm. Repeat with the remaining butter and bread cubes. Thread the bread cubes, banana slices, blueberries and raspberries alternately onto twelve wooden skewers. Serve immediately with maple syrup, if desired.

Note: Pullman bread (pain de mie) works wonderfully in this recipe.

Hadley Upchurch Scott

When I moved to Columbus as a nervous young bride, I was 'specially worried about being accepted by the friends of my husband's large family. Well, you can imagine my utter delight at receiving a luncheon invitation by mail from the lovely and highly esteemed Mrs. William Zimmerman. When the day of the event finally came, I spent the whole morning getting ready—a new spring dress, long gloves, and a fetching little hat. Approaching her driveway, I was shocked that no other cars were arriving; surely no female in her right mind would decline this gracious invitation! My trembling hand rang the bell and after an agonizing moment Mrs. Zimmerman herself opened the door wearing a bathrobe and a fleetingly startled expression.

"Oh, Dorothy, dahlin', the luncheon's tomorrow," she said. "But I was just finishing up in the kitchen, so come on in, pull up a chair, and we'll have a pimento cheese sandwich and a little visit." I was absolutely mortified. But being the brazen, thoughtless, naïve nineteen-year-old that I was, I felt no qualms about accepting her kind invitation, and it never crossed my mind that she may have had more important things to do. I ended up having a wonderful visit with this bundle of charm. And at the real luncheon the next day, she was kind enough to treat me as if she hadn't seen me in weeks!

—Dorothy McNeel Young

Buttermilk Biscuits

Serves 9

To ensure tall and flaky biscuits, butter and buttermilk should be kept cold until use. Place biscuits in a preheated oven immediately after cutting.

1 cup (2 sticks) salted butter
2 cups self-rising flour
3/4 cup buttermilk
Melted butter for brushing

Cut 1 cup butter into the flour with a pastry blender until the crumbs are the size of peas. Add the buttermilk and stir with a fork to form a dough. Place on a floured surface. Knead several times with floured hands. Pat into a circle 3/4 inch thick. Cut with a 2-inch biscuit cutter. Place on a baking sheet or baking stone. Repeat with any remaining dough. Bake at 425 degrees for 12 minutes or until light brown. Brush the tops with butter.

Katherine Ramsey Maxey

Cheese Garlic Biscuits

Serves 9

2 cups baking mix
2/3 cup milk
1/2 cup (2 ounces) shredded Cheddar cheese
2 tablespoons butter or margarine, melted
1/8 teaspoon garlic powder

Combine the baking mix, milk and cheese in a bowl and mix to form a soft dough. Drop nine spoonfuls of dough onto an ungreased baking sheet. Bake at 450 degrees for 8 to 10 minutes or until golden brown. Mix the butter and garlic powder in a small bowl. Brush over the warm biscuits.

Amy Johnson Bickerstaff

Blueberry Muffins

Serves 12

1 egg
1/2 cup milk
1/4 cup vegetable oil
11/2 cups all-purpose flour
1/2 cup sugar
2 teaspoons baking powder
1/2 teaspoon salt
1 cup fresh or frozen blueberries

Beat the egg in a mixing bowl. Add the milk and oil and mix well. Stir in the flour, sugar, baking powder and salt. Fold in the blueberries. Fill greased and floured muffin cups two-thirds full. Bake at 400 degrees for 20 minutes or until brown.

Lisa Lane White

Bran Muffins

Serves 22

1/2 cup boiling water
3 cups 100% bran cereal
21/2 cups all-purpose flour
21/2 teaspoons baking soda
1 teaspoon salt
1 cup (2 sticks) margarine, softened
11/2 cups sugar or honey
2 eggs
2 cups buttermilk

Pour the boiling water over 1 cup of the cereal in a bowl and set aside. Mix the flour, baking soda and salt together. Cream the margarine and sugar in a mixing bowl. Add the eggs and mix well. Add the buttermilk and mix well. Stir in the remaining 2 cups cereal. Add the flour mixture and mix well. Stir in the moistened cereal. Spoon into muffin cups. Bake at 375 degrees for 20 minutes.

Beth Foster Thomas

Sour Cream Muffins

Serves 24

1 cup (2 sticks) butter or margarine, softened
1 cup sour cream
2 cups self-rising flour

Combine the butter with the sour cream and flour in a bowl and mix well. Spoon into ungreased miniature muffin cups. Bake at 400 degrees for 12 to 15 minutes or until light brown.

Note: For variation, add 1 cup shredded Cheddar cheese. These muffins freeze well.

Eleanor Glenn Hardegree

Fluffy Blueberry Pancakes

Serves 4 or 5

1 3/4 cups all-purpose flour
2 teaspoons baking soda
1 teaspoon salt
2 tablespoons sugar
1 egg yolk
1/2 cup unsweetened applesauce
1 teaspoon vanilla extract
3/4 to 1 cup skim milk
4 egg whites, stiffly beaten
Blueberries

Mix the flour, baking soda and salt together. Mix the sugar, egg yolk, applesauce, vanilla and milk in a bowl. Stir in the flour mixture. Fold in the egg whites. Pour 1/4 cup at a time onto a hot greased griddle. Sprinkle about 5 or 6 blueberries evenly on each pancake. Cook until brown on both sides, turning once.

Jerry Floyd Jones

Puffy Pancake

Serves 4

As an alternative, substitute the juice of a tangerine, clementine, or mandarin orange for the lemon or lime juice.

1/2 cup (1 stick) butter
4 eggs
1 cup milk
1 teaspoon vanilla extract
1/2 teaspoon almond extract
1 cup all-purpose flour
Juice of 1/2 lemon or lime
Confectioners' sugar for sprinkling

Bake the butter in a large baking dish at 425 degrees until melted, watching carefully to prevent burning. Beat the eggs in a mixing bowl until frothy. Add the milk, vanilla and almond extract. Stir in the flour just until moistened. Pour into the hot butter. Bake for 15 minutes or until the pancake rises and becomes puffy. Drizzle with the lemon juice. Sprinkle with confectioners' sugar. Serve immediately.

Teresa Carswell Howard

Chipley Waffles

Serves 4 to 6

2 eggs
1 1/4 cups milk
2 cups all-purpose flour
1/2 cup vegetable oil
2 tablespoons sugar
4 teaspoons baking powder
1 teaspoon salt

Beat the eggs well in a bowl. Add the milk and flour and beat well. Add the oil, sugar, baking powder and salt and mix well. Cook in a waffle iron using the manufacturer's directions.

Jerry Floyd Jones

Cranberry Scones

Serves 10

For a sweeter version, use chocolate chips instead of the dried cranberries.

2 cups all-purpose flour $^1/_2$ teaspoon salt
$^1/_4$ cup sugar 3 to 4 ounces dried cranberries
$2^1/_2$ teaspoons baking powder $1^1/_4$ cups heavy cream

Whisk the flour, sugar, baking powder, salt and cranberries in a bowl until well mixed. Make a well in the center and add the cream. Fold four to five times from the side of the bowl to the center with a fork. Pat the dough on a floured surface. Cut into wedges. Place on a baking sheet lined with baking parchment. Bake at 425 degrees for 12 to 15 minutes or until brown.

Mary Helen Peacock, Charleston, South Carolina

Brunch Coffee Cake

Serves 8 to 10

2 (8-count) cans refrigerator crescent rolls	2 egg whites, stiffly beaten
1 cup (or less) sugar	1/2 cup sugar
16 ounces cream cheese, softened	1 tablespoon cinnamon
2 egg yolks	1/2 cup almonds or pecans (optional)

Unroll one can of the crescent roll dough in a greased 9×13-inch baking dish, pressing the perforations to seal. Cream 1 cup sugar, the cream cheese and egg yolks in a mixing bowl. Spread over the crescent roll dough. Unroll the remaining can of crescent roll dough and press the perforations to seal. Place over the cream cheese layer. Spread the egg whites over the dough. Mix 1/2 cup sugar, the cinnamon and almonds in a bowl. Sprinkle over the top. Bake at 350 degrees for 35 minutes or until brown. Let stand for a few minutes before serving or the cream cheese will be gooey.

Marietta Rushton O'Neill

Blueberry Breakfast Cake

Serves 12 to 15

The cake can be made a day ahead, chilled, and baked at 350 degrees for 15 minutes or until warm before pouring the hot mixture over the cake.

1 (2-layer) package white cake mix	2 cups sugar
3 eggs	1 cup half-and-half
2 cups fresh blueberries	2 teaspoons vanilla extract
1 cup (2 sticks) butter	1 cup fresh blueberries

Prepare the cake mix using the package directions, using 3 whole eggs. Mix well. Fold in 2 cups blueberries. Spoon into a greased 9×13-inch glass cake pan. Bake at 350 degrees using the package directions.

Melt the butter in a small saucepan. Stir in the sugar, half-and-half and vanilla. Cook over medium-low heat for 10 minutes or until the sugar dissolves, stirring constantly. Pour over the hot cake. Top with 1 cup blueberries. Serve while the cake is still warm.

Shannan Hartley Bickerstaff

Blueberry Streusel Coffee Cake

Serves 10

This recipe combines three "great for you" ingredients...blueberries, walnuts, and whole wheat flour.

1 tablespoon unsalted butter
2 tablespoons all-purpose flour
1/4 cup packed light brown sugar
1 teaspoon cinnamon
1/2 cup walnuts
1/2 cup canola oil
1/2 cup packed light brown sugar
1/2 cup granulated sugar
2 eggs

1 teaspoon vanilla extract
1 cup unbleached all-purpose flour
1 cup whole wheat flour
1 teaspoon baking powder
1 teaspoon baking soda
1/4 teaspoon salt
1 cup buttermilk or low-fat plain yogurt
2 cups fresh blueberries

Process the butter, 2 tablespoons all-purpose flour, 1/4 cup brown sugar, the cinnamon and walnuts in a food processor to form coarse crumbs. Set aside to use for the topping.

Beat the canola oil, 1/2 cup brown sugar, the granulated sugar, eggs and vanilla in a mixing bowl until smooth. Add 1 cup all-purpose flour, the whole wheat flour, baking powder, baking soda and salt and mix well. Add the buttermilk and beat until smooth. Spoon into a lightly buttered and floured 9-inch springform pan. Sprinkle the blueberries over the top and swirl into the batter. Sprinkle the topping evenly over the batter. Bake at 350 degrees for 35 to 40 minutes or until golden brown. Cool in the pan on a wire rack for 10 minutes. Cut into wedges and serve.

Charlene Roberts Marx

"*I*t isn't so much what's on the table that matters, as what's on the chairs."

—*William S. Gilbert*

Monkey Bread

Serves 8 to 10

1/2 cup pecans, chopped
1/2 cup granulated sugar
1 tablespoon cinnamon

3 (10-count) cans refrigerator biscuits
1/2 cup (1 stick) butter
1 cup packed brown sugar

Sprinkle the pecans in a greased bundt pan. Mix the granulated sugar and cinnamon in a bowl. Cut the biscuits into quarters and roll in the cinnamon-sugar. Place in the prepared pan. Melt the butter and brown sugar in a saucepan over low heat, stirring frequently. Pour over the biscuit quarters. Bake at 350 degrees for 30 minutes.

Dori Sponcler Jones

Sour Cream Coffee Cake

Serves 12

8 teaspoons sugar
2 teaspoons cinnamon
2 cups (4 sticks) butter, softened
4 cups sugar
4 eggs
2 cups sour cream

1 teaspoon vanilla extract
2 teaspoons baking powder
1/2 teaspoon salt
4 cups all-purpose flour, sifted
2 cups chopped pecans

Mix 8 teaspoons sugar and the cinnamon in a bowl. Cream the butter and 4 cups sugar in a mixing bowl. Add the eggs one at a time, beating well after each addition until fluffy. Add the sour cream, vanilla, baking powder and salt and mix well. Fold in the flour. Divide one-half of the batter among three greased round cake pans. Top with 1 cup of the pecans. Sprinkle with one-half of the cinnamon-sugar. Spread with the remaining batter. Sprinkle with the remaining 1 cup pecans and remaining cinnamon-sugar. Bake at 350 degrees for 35 to 40 minutes or until brown on top.

Note: Increase the baking time if baking all three coffee cakes at one time.

Marietta Rushton O'Neill

Yia Yia's Apple Plum Bread

Serves 16

*This bread smells delicious while baking and is perfect on a cool fall day.
Keep one loaf for your family and take the other loaf to a friend or neighbor.*

3 eggs
2 cups sugar
1 cup vegetable oil
2 (4-ounce) jars apple and plum baby food
2 cups self-rising flour

1 teaspoon cinnamon
1 cup chopped pecans
1 1/2 cups confectioners' sugar
6 tablespoons orange juice

Beat the eggs lightly in a large bowl. Add the sugar, oil, baby food, flour, cinnamon and pecans and mix by hand until blended. Pour into two greased 4×8-inch loaf pans, filling each about one-half full. Bake at 350 degrees for 45 minutes or until a wooden pick inserted in the center comes out clean.

Combine the confectioners' sugar and orange juice in a bowl and mix until smooth. Pour over the warm loaves in the loaf pans. Let stand until cool.

Shannan Hartley Bickerstaff

Classic Banana Bread

Serves 8 to 12

2 cups all-purpose flour
1 teaspoon baking soda
1 teaspoon salt
1/2 cup (1 stick) butter, softened
1 cup sugar

2 eggs
3 very ripe large bananas, mashed
1 teaspoon vanilla extract
1 cup pecans, coarsely chopped

Mix the flour, baking soda and salt in a bowl. Cream the butter and sugar in a mixing bowl. Add the eggs one at a time, mixing well after each addition. Stir in the bananas and vanilla. Add the flour mixture gradually, beating well after each addition. Fold in the pecans. Pour into a greased 5×9-inch loaf pan. Let stand for 20 minutes. Bake at 350 degrees for 50 minutes.

Teresa Carswell Howard

Gingerbread with Warm Lemon Sauce

Serves 9

Gingerbread

1 1/2 cups all-purpose flour
1 teaspoon baking soda
1/2 teaspoon salt
1 teaspoon ginger
1/2 teaspoon cinnamon
1/4 teaspoon ground cloves
1/8 teaspoon nutmeg
1 egg
1/2 cup sugar
1 teaspoon vanilla extract

1/2 cup each molasses and boiling water
1/2 cup vegetable oil

Lemon Sauce

1/2 cup sugar
2 tablespoons cornstarch
1/4 teaspoon salt
1 cup boiling water
1 teaspoon lemon zest
1/4 cup lemon juice
2 tablespoons butter

To prepare the gingerbread, mix the flour, baking soda, salt, ginger, cinnamon, cloves and nutmeg together. Beat the egg, sugar, vanilla and molasses in a mixing bowl. Stir in the flour mixture. Add the boiling water and oil and mix well. Pour into a greased and floured 8×8-inch baking pan. Bake at 350 degrees for 35 to 40 minutes or until the bread tests done.

To prepare the lemon sauce, mix the sugar, cornstarch and salt in a saucepan. Add the boiling water. Bring to a boil over low heat. Cook for 10 minutes or until clear and thickened, stirring constantly. Remove from the heat. Stir in the lemon zest, lemon juice and butter. Serve warm with the gingerbread.

Shannan Hartley Bickerstaff

Strawberry Bread

Serves 20

1 1/4 cups vegetable oil
3 eggs
2 cups sugar
3 cups all-purpose flour
1 tablespoon cinnamon

1 teaspoon baking soda
1 teaspoon salt
2 (10-ounce) packages frozen sliced
    strawberries, thawed and drained
1 cup chopped pecans

Mix the oil, eggs and sugar in a bowl. Stir in a mixture of the flour, cinnamon, baking soda and salt. Stir in the strawberries and pecans. Bake in two greased and floured loaf pans at 350 degrees for 1 hour.

Laura Schomburg Patrick

Corn Bread Dressing

Serves 16

4 cups crumbled corn bread	2 eggs, beaten
3 cups crumbled biscuits	1/2 cup (1 stick) margarine, melted
5 slices white bread, torn	1/2 cup chopped fresh parsley
4 cups chicken broth	2 teaspoons dried thyme
3/4 cup water	2 teaspoons dried sage
1 1/2 cups chopped celery	1 teaspoon dried rosemary
3/4 cup chopped onion	Salt and pepper to taste

Mix the corn bread, biscuits and bread in a large bowl. Add the broth, water, celery, onion, eggs, margarine, parsley, thyme, sage, rosemary, salt and pepper and mix well. Pour into a greased 9×13-inch baking dish. Bake at 400 degrees for 50 to 55 minutes or until a tester inserted in the center comes out clean.

Mattie West Paris

Corn Bread

Serves 8

1 egg
1/3 cup vegetable oil
2 cups buttermilk
1 1/2 cups self-rising cornmeal
Pinch of salt

Mix the egg, oil and buttermilk in a bowl. Stir in the cornmeal and salt. Pour into a well-greased 10-inch cast-iron skillet. Place in a cold oven. Set the oven temperature at 450 degrees and bake for 15 to 20 minutes or until the bread tests done.

Sara Hatcher Dismuke

Broccoli Bread

Serves 12

This is good enough to be dessert.

1 (10-ounce) package frozen chopped broccoli, thawed and drained
1 large onion, chopped
4 eggs, beaten
1/2 cup (1 stick) margarine, melted
2 cups (8 ounces) shredded sharp Cheddar cheese
1 teaspoon salt
1 (8-ounce) package corn bread mix

Combine the broccoli, onion, eggs, margarine, cheese, salt and corn bread mix in a bowl in the order listed and mix well with a spoon. Spoon into a greased 9×13-inch baking pan. Bake at 400 degrees for 20 minutes.

Sandy Tally Coolik

Garlic Bread

Serves 8

1/2 cup (1 stick) butter, melted
3 garlic cloves, pressed
1 loaf French bread
2 tablespoons chopped fresh parsley

Mix the butter and garlic in a bowl. Cut the bread into halves lengthwise. Place crust side down on a rimmed baking sheet. Pour the butter mixture over the bread, spreading the garlic evenly. Sprinkle with the parsley. Bake at 400 degrees for 10 minutes. Cut into slices and serve hot.

Edie Pendleton Evans

From Folding Chairs to Fanbacks

Soups, Salads & Sandwiches

If our streets could talk, they would voice sentiments of a town that has seen many cultural, visual, and aerial changes: a passion-filled community that continuously strives to preserve the past and honor its forebears, yet welcomes new families with open seats and generous gestures. As a part of the continuing revitalization of Uptown Columbus, these "City of Columbus" iron benches are a part of the new streetscape improvements along Broadway.

—Elizabeth Barker

Historic Columbus Foundation

From Folding Chairs to Fanbacks

Soups, Salads & Sandwiches

Italian Chicken Soup

Serves 8

A sick-day favorite.

10 cups water
4 ribs celery, cut into large pieces
4 sprigs of fresh parsley
2 carrots, cut into large pieces
2 garlic cloves, minced
2 cloves
1 leek, trimmed and cut into large pieces
2 bay leaves
1 (3- to 5-pound) chicken
6 tablespoons uncooked pastina
2 tablespoons freshly grated Parmesan cheese
1 teaspoon salt
1/4 teaspoon pepper
1 teaspoon Nature's Seasons seasoning blend
1 tablespoon Worcestershire sauce
2 eggs, beaten

Bring the water, celery, parsley, carrots, garlic, cloves, leek, bay leaves and chicken to a low boil in a stockpot. Cover and reduce the heat. Simmer for 1 1/2 to 2 hours. Remove from the heat to cool. Remove the chicken, celery, carrots and leeks. Shred the chicken, discarding the skin and bones. Chop the celery, carrots and leeks. Strain the broth, discarding the solids.

Bring 8 to 9 cups of the broth, the chopped vegetables and chicken to a low boil in a Dutch oven. Add the pasta, cheese, salt, pepper, seasoning blend and Worcestershire sauce. Cook for 3 minutes. Drizzle in the eggs, stirring constantly. Remove from the heat immediately. Ladle into soup bowls.

Gardiner Zollo Church

Chicken and Rice Soup

Serves 6 to 8

1 (3- to 4-pound) chicken
2 (15-ounce) cans chicken broth
6 cloves
1 onion, cut into halves
2 carrots, chopped
5 garlic cloves

10 peppercorns
1 large bay leaf
2 ribs celery, chopped
3 cups steamed rice
1/4 cup flat-leaf parsley, chopped

Place the chicken in a stockpot with the broth. Add enough water to cover the chicken. Stud the cloves in each onion half. Add the studded onion, carrots, garlic, peppercorns, bay leaf and celery to the chicken. Bring to a boil over medium-high heat and reduce the heat. Simmer for 45 minutes or until the chicken pulls away from the bone. Remove the chicken to a platter and let stand until cool enough to handle. Strain the broth, discarding the solids. Cut the chicken into bite-size pieces, discarding the skin and bones. Return the strained broth to the stockpot. Add the chicken and rice. Simmer until heated through. Ladle into soup bowls. Sprinkle with the parsley.

Julie McCullough Pendleton, Smiths, Alabama

Clam Chowder

Serves 6 to 8

1 (10-ounce) can whole shelled clams
1 tablespoon margarine
1/3 cup chopped celery
1/3 cup chopped onion
1 1/4 cups chopped peeled potatoes
1 tablespoon cornstarch
1 cup skim milk

1 (12-ounce) can evaporated skim milk
5 slices bacon, cooked and crumbled
1/2 teaspoon salt
1/8 teaspoon pepper
Hot pepper sauce to taste
Several dashes of paprika

Drain the clams, reserving 1/2 cup of the liquid. Combine the reserved clam liquid, margarine, celery, onion and potatoes in a large saucepan. Bring to a boil and reduce the heat. Simmer, covered, until the potatoes are tender. Stir the cornstarch into the skim milk and evaporated skim milk in a bowl. Add to the potato mixture. Add the clams, bacon, salt, pepper, hot sauce and paprika. Cook over medium heat until thickened, stirring constantly. Ladle into soup bowls.

Jennifer Gillespie Daniel

Onion Soup

Serves 8 to 10

5 large Spanish onions, thinly sliced	Salt and pepper to taste
3 tablespoons butter	2 tablespoons brandy
1 tablespoon vegetable oil	8 to 10 thick slices French bread
1 teaspoon salt	Melted butter for brushing
1/4 teaspoon sugar	8 to 10 teaspoons grated Parmesan cheese
3 tablespoons all-purpose flour	Cayenne pepper to taste
2 quarts beef stock or bouillon	8 to 10 tablespoons shredded Swiss cheese
1/2 cup dry white wine	Melted butter for drizzling

Combine the onions, 3 tablespoons butter and the oil in a heavy saucepan. Cook, covered, over low heat for 15 minutes. Uncover and increase the heat to medium. Add 1 teaspoon salt and the sugar. Cook for 30 to 40 minutes or until brown. Sprinkle with the flour. Cook for 2 minutes. Add the stock, wine and salt and pepper to taste. Simmer, partially covered, for 30 to 40 minutes. Add the brandy. (The soup may be made ahead to this point.)

Brush each side of the bread with melted butter. Sprinkle each with 1 teaspoon Parmesan cheese and the cayenne pepper. Place in the bottom of each ovenproof serving bowl. Ladle the soup into the bowls. The bread will float to the top. Sprinkle each with 1 tablespoon Swiss cheese. Drizzle with melted butter. Bake at 400 degrees until brown.

Mary King Smalley, Griffin, Georgia

One of the most appealing and well-loved tables I have ever seen was in a charming early nineteenth-century farmhouse used and enjoyed by Gin and Spencer Waddell during the 1940s and '50s. It was a long, thick pine table with four sturdy legs. On its surface were carved—yes, literally carved—names, initials, and dates which family members and friends had left as eternal reminders of happy times. Friends gathered 'round this wonderful old table as a ritual on Sunday nights— no invitation was needed or expected. There was always a crowd and somehow always enough delicious food. The relationships established and nourished here lasted a lifetime!

—Cynthia Young Bowman

Gazpacho

Serves 6 to 8

1 (48-ounce) can tomato juice	1 1/2 tablespoons sugar
1 (56-ounce) can diced tomatoes	1 teaspoon garlic salt
2 large cucumbers, peeled and chopped	1/2 teaspoon celery salt
2 large green bell peppers, chopped	1/2 teaspoon pepper
1 bunch green onions, chopped	Juice of 1 lemon
1/2 cup red wine vinegar	Sour cream for garnish
2 or 3 drops of Tabasco sauce	

Combine the tomato juice, tomatoes, cucumbers, bell peppers, green onions, vinegar, Tabasco sauce, sugar, garlic salt, celery salt, pepper and lemon juice in a large container. Chill, covered, for 3 to 10 hours. Ladle into soup bowls and garnish with sour cream.

Martha Gilliam Hatcher

Classic Vichyssoise

Serves 6 to 8

Omit the wine and add another cup of chicken broth, if desired.

4 leeks	1 teaspoon salt
6 tablespoons butter	1 teaspoon white pepper
4 potatoes, peeled and sliced	1 cup heavy cream
3 cups chicken broth	Chopped fresh chives or green onions
1 cup white wine	for garnish

Rinse the leeks well. Discard the green tops and cut the white portions into 1-inch slices. Sauté the leeks in the butter in a saucepan until tender and translucent. Add the potatoes, broth, wine, salt and white pepper. Bring to a boil and reduce the heat. Simmer for 30 to 45 minutes or until the potatoes are falling apart. Remove from the heat and cool slightly. Purée the soup with an immersion blender. Stir in the cream. Ladle into soup bowls. Garnish with chives. Serve the soup hot or chilled.

Teresa Carswell Howard

One Potato, Two Potato Soup

Serves 6

This is popular with the children, too.

1 quart chicken broth
1 (32-ounce) package frozen cubed hash brown potatoes
1 (14-ounce) can cream of chicken soup
8 ounces cream cheese
1/2 cup (2 ounces) shredded Cheddar cheese
1/2 cup sour cream
1/2 cup chopped green onions

Combine the broth, potatoes and soup in a large slow cooker. Cook on Low for 4 hours, stirring occasionally. Cut the cream cheese into cubes and add to the soup. Cook on High until the cream cheese melts, stirring occasionally. Continue to cook for 30 minutes. Ladle into soup bowls. Top with the Cheddar cheese, sour cream and green onions.

Allison Weaver Peak

Taco Soup

Serves 10

Serve with a slice of corn bread and you have an easy weeknight meal.

1 pound ground beef
1 onion, chopped
1 envelope taco seasoning mix
1 envelope ranch salad dressing mix
1 (10-ounce) can tomatoes with green chiles
1 (15-ounce) can diced tomatoes
1 (15-ounce) can kidney beans
1 (15-ounce) can black beans
1 (15-ounce) can pinto beans
1 (15-ounce) can whole kernel white corn
1 (8-ounce) jar taco sauce
1 (10-ounce) can fat-free chicken broth
Shredded cheese for garnish
Fat-free sour cream for garnish

Brown the ground beef with the onion in a large saucepan, stirring until the ground beef is crumbly; drain. Add the taco seasoning mix and salad dressing mix and mix well. Add the undrained vegetables, taco sauce and broth and mix well. Bring to a low boil and cook for 5 minutes. Ladle into soup bowls. Garnish with cheese and sour cream.

Martha Gilliam Hatcher

Vegetable Soup

Serves 8 to 10

1 soup bone with some meat	Cabbage (optional)
1/4 cup vegetable oil	1 cup sliced carrots
4 cups water	1 cup sliced celery
1 onion, chopped	1 tablespoon salt
1 (28-ounce) can tomatoes, chopped	2 sprigs of fresh parsley, finely chopped
2 cups green beans	2 bay leaves, crumbled
2 cups whole kernel corn	5 peppercorns
2 cups peas	1/2 teaspoon thyme
2 cups chopped potatoes	1/2 teaspoon marjoram
2 cups sliced okra	

Cut the meat from the soup bone. Brown the meat with the bone in the oil in a large stockpot.
Add the water. Cook over low heat for 2 1/2 hours. Add the onion, tomatoes, green beans, corn, peas,
potatoes, okra, cabbage, carrots, celery, salt, parsley, bay leaves, peppercorns, thyme and marjoram.
Cook for 30 to 60 minutes, adding water as needed for the desired consistency. Ladle into soup bowls.

Lenore Abbott Hilbert, Dothan, Alabama

Chicken and Black Bean Tortilla Soup

Serves 6

1 red bell pepper
1½ cups frozen whole kernel corn
3 tablespoons vegetable oil
1 pound chicken tenders, chopped
1 teaspoon poultry seasoning
1 teaspoon ground cumin
Salt and pepper to taste
1 zucchini, chopped
1 squash, chopped
1 yellow onion, chopped
3 garlic cloves, chopped

1 or 2 canned chipotle chiles, chopped
1 (28-ounce) can stewed tomatoes
1 (8-ounce) can tomato sauce
3 cups chicken stock
1 (15-ounce) can black beans,
    drained and rinsed
Shredded cheese for garnish
Sour cream for garnish
Chopped green onions for garnish
Chopped avocado for garnish
Tortilla chips for garnish

Line a broiler pan with foil and grease the foil. Remove the stem and seeds from the bell pepper. Cut the bell pepper into quarters and flatten. Place on the prepared pan. Bake at 425 degrees for 10 to 15 minutes or until charred. Place in a container with a lid. Let stand, covered, until cool. Remove the charred skin and chop the bell pepper. Thaw the corn in a colander with warm water. Spread the corn on the prepared pan and drizzle with 1 tablespoon of the oil. Bake for 10 minutes and set aside.

Heat the remaining 2 tablespoons oil in a stockpot. Add the chicken, poultry seasoning, cumin, salt and pepper. Cook until the chicken is light brown on each side. Add the zucchini, squash, onion, garlic and chipotle chiles. Cook for 5 to 7 minutes or until the vegetables are soft. Add the tomatoes, tomato sauce and stock. Bring to a boil and reduce the heat to medium-low. Stir in the chopped roasted bell pepper, roasted corn and beans. Cook until heated through, stirring gently. Ladle into soup bowls. Garnish with shredded cheese, sour cream, green onions, avocado and tortilla chips.

Note: This recipe can be easily doubled. It can be made ahead and freezes well.

Mary Lynn Pugh Grubb

Bladen Pharmacy's Chili

Serves 20

5 pounds ground chuck	2 (4-ounce) cans chopped green chiles
21/2 large onions, finely chopped	21/2 cups chili powder
4 (16-ounce) cans chili beans	6 tablespoons Accent
21/2 (28-ounce) cans crushed tomatoes	1/4 cup ground cumin

Brown the ground chuck with the onions in a stockpot, stirring until the ground chuck is crumbly; drain. Add the undrained chili beans, tomatoes, green chiles, chili powder, Accent and cumin and mix well. Simmer over low heat for 1 hour, stirring frequently to prevent sticking. Ladle into soup bowls.

Kelly Bladen McKinstry

I have the fondest memories of sitting at the soda fountain on the end bar stool at Bladen Pharmacy as a little girl. It was interesting to turn around on the stool and watch my dad fill prescriptions and answer customers' questions while I ate my lunch. After school, I always enjoyed sitting on my bar stool finishing my homework, reading magazines, and visiting with our customers.

— Kelly Bladen McKinstry

Brunswick Stew

Serves 6 to 8

This is a versatile recipe, as the ingredients and/or their proportions can be altered to taste.

2 cups shredded cooked chicken

2 cups chopped barbecued beef or ribs (optional)

1 (24-ounce) can Brunswick stew

1 (28-ounce) can petite diced tomatoes

2 cups frozen butter beans

2 cups frozen corn

4 cups chicken broth

2 tablespoons Worcestershire sauce

1/2 bottle favorite barbecue sauce, or more to taste

3 tablespoons lemon juice, or juice of 2 lemons

Salt and pepper to taste

Combine the chicken, beef, canned Brunswick stew, tomatoes, beans, corn, broth, Worcestershire sauce, barbecue sauce, lemon juice, salt and pepper in a large saucepan and mix well. Bring to a low boil. Cook for 10 to 15 minutes. Reduce the heat to low. Simmer for 1 hour or until the vegetables are tender, stirring occasionally. Ladle into soup bowls.

Note: You can use a lemon pepper rotisserie chicken.

Dradyn Coolik Hinson

My parents take care of my daughter Shelby frequently. Sometimes during her visit with them, she decides that my father, her "Big Daddy," needs a haircut. He gladly complies and moves a kitchen chair into the den, where she cuts away to her heart's content. He doesn't have much hair to cut, but she works diligently to get it right! My mother smiles, shakes her head, and cleans up the mess. Both know they are creating a special memory for Shelby.

—Joy Bowick Wells

One-Hundred-Dollar Chili

Serves 36

1 cup chopped onion
1/2 cup good-quality olive oil
8 pounds ground chuck
1 pound sweet Italian sausage
1 pound hot bulk sausage
2 (12-ounce) cans tomato paste
1/2 cup chili powder
1/2 cup Dijon mustard
6 tablespoons ground cumin
1/4 cup dried basil
1/4 cup dried oregano
1/4 cup salt
3 tablespoons minced garlic cloves
2 tablespoons freshly ground pepper
1/2 cup dry red wine
1/4 cup lemon juice
5 (32-ounce) cans Italian plum tomatoes
1/2 cup chopped fresh dill weed
1/2 cup chopped parsley
6 (16-ounce) cans kidney beans, drained

Sauté the onion in the olive oil in a large stockpot for 10 minutes. Add the ground chuck, Italian sausage and bulk sausage. Cook until brown, stirring until crumbly; drain. Stir in the tomato paste, chili powder, Dijon mustard, cumin, basil, oregano, salt, garlic and pepper. Cook over low heat for 10 minutes, stirring frequently. Add the wine, lemon juice, undrained tomatoes, dill weed, parsley and beans. Simmer, covered, for 20 minutes. Ladle into soup bowls. Serve with sour cream, chives and shredded Cheddar cheese, if desired.

Note: This recipe can be halved.

Carolyn Zollo Crenshaw, Spartanburg, South Carolina

Arugula and Spinach Salad with Roasted Asparagus

Serves 4 to 6

Shallot Vinaigrette
1/4 cup minced shallots
2 tablespoons fresh lemon juice
3 tablespoons red wine vinegar
2 teaspoons grated lemon zest
2 teaspoons Dijon mustard
1/3 cup extra-virgin olive oil
Salt and freshly cracked pepper to taste

Salad
11/2 pounds asparagus, trimmed
Honey to taste
6 cups lightly packed arugula
2 cups lightly packed spinach
Salt and freshly cracked pepper to taste
1/2 cup (2 ounces) freshly grated Parmesan cheese

To prepare the vinaigrette, whisk the shallots, lemon juice, vinegar, lemon zest and Dijon mustard in a small bowl until mixed. Whisk in the olive oil gradually. Add salt and pepper. Chill, covered, in the refrigerator.

To prepare the salad, place the asparagus on a rimmed baking sheet. Drizzle with honey. Roast at 400 degrees until tender-crisp. Combine the arugula, spinach and roasted asparagus in a large bowl. Add the vinaigrette and toss to coat. Sprinkle with salt, pepper and cheese. Serve immediately.

Millie Peacock Patrick

Blueberry Spinach Salad

Serves 4

Dijon Vinaigrette
1/4 cup light olive oil
1/4 cup raspberry vinegar
2 teaspoons Dijon mustard
1 teaspoon sugar
1/2 teaspoon salt

Salad
10 ounces fresh spinach
4 ounces blue cheese, crumbled
1 cup fresh blueberries, rinsed and drained
1/2 cup pecans, toasted and chopped

To prepare the vinaigrette, whisk the olive oil, vinegar, Dijon mustard, sugar and salt in a bowl until blended.

To prepare the salad, combine the spinach, cheese, blueberries and pecans in a salad bowl. Add the vinaigrette and toss to coat.

Donna Sears Hand

Asian Coleslaw

Serves 8 to 12

Always a hit with everyone, especially men.

2 (3-ounce) packages oriental-flavor ramen noodles
1 (1-pound) package coleslaw
1 cup sliced almonds
1 cup sunflower seeds
2 bunches green onions, sliced
1/3 cup vegetable oil
1/2 cup sugar
1/3 cup white vinegar
1/3 cup applesauce

Crumble the ramen noodles and place in a large bowl, reserving the seasoning packets. Add the coleslaw, almonds, sunflower seeds and green onions and toss well. Combine the contents of the reserved seasoning packets, oil, sugar, vinegar and applesauce in a bowl and mix well. Pour over the coleslaw mixture and toss to coat. Marinate, covered, in the refrigerator for 2 to 3 hours before serving.

Libby Carter Hudson

Coleslaw

Serves 10

1 head cabbage
1/2 cup chopped onion
1 teaspoon celery seeds
1/3 cup sweet green pickle relish
3/4 cup mayonnaise, or to taste

Cut the cabbage into quarters. Cut each quarter into 2-inch cubes. Pulse one layer of cabbage cubes at a time at quick intervals in a food processor until chopped. Do not finely chop. Combine the chopped cabbage, onion, celery seeds, relish and mayonnaise in a large bowl and toss to mix. Chill, covered, until serving time.

Julie Hattaway Hinson

Cornucopia Salad

Serves 6

½ cup walnuts
3 to 4 tablespoons butter, melted (optional)
1 package mixed salad greens
1 package romaine lettuce, torn into
bite-size pieces
½ cup dried cranberries
1 cup blue cheese crumbles

1 Granny Smith apple, chopped
4 green onions, sliced
¼ cup vegetable oil
2 tablespoons sugar
2 tablespoons apple cider vinegar
½ teaspoon salt
1 teaspoon pepper

Place the walnuts on a baking sheet. Brush with the butter. Bake at 350 degrees for 20 minutes or until toasted, watching carefully to prevent overbrowning. Combine the salad greens, lettuce, cranberries, cheese crumbles, toasted walnuts, apple and green onions in a large bowl. Whisk the oil, sugar, vinegar, salt and pepper in a glass bowl. Pour over the salad and toss to coat.

Dori Sponcler Jones

Grape Salad

Serves 12 to 14

1 cup sour cream
8 ounces cream cheese, softened
½ cup granulated sugar
3 cups white grapes
3 cups red grapes
1 cup packed brown sugar
1 cup chopped pecans

Combine the sour cream, cream cheese and granulated sugar in a large bowl and mix well. Add the white grapes and red grapes and stir to coat. Place in a large serving bowl. Mix the brown sugar and pecans in a bowl. Sprinkle over the top of the grape mixture. Chill, covered, for 8 to 10 hours.

Tiffany Kitchens Wilson

Hearts of Palm Salad

Serves 8 to 10

Oriental Vinaigrette
1/2 cup vegetable oil
1/4 cup sugar
1/4 cup rice wine vinegar
1 tablespoon soy sauce
1/2 teaspoon salt
1/4 teaspoon pepper

Salad
1 (3-ounce) package ramen noodles
1/4 cup (1/2 stick) butter
1 cup chopped walnuts
1 head romaine lettuce, torn into
   bite-size pieces
1 bunch green onions, chopped
1 (14-ounce) can sliced
   hearts of palm, drained

To prepare the vinaigrette, whisk the oil, sugar, vinegar, soy sauce, salt and pepper in a bowl until the sugar dissolves.

To prepare the salad, crumble the ramen noodles, reserving the seasoning packet for another use. Melt the butter in a skillet over medium heat. Add the walnuts and ramen noodles. Cook until toasted, stirring frequently. Remove to paper towels to drain. Combine the lettuce, green onions, hearts of palm and toasted walnut mixture in a large salad bowl and toss to mix. Add the vinaigrette and toss to coat.

Carolyn Zollo Crenshaw, Spartanburg, South Carolina

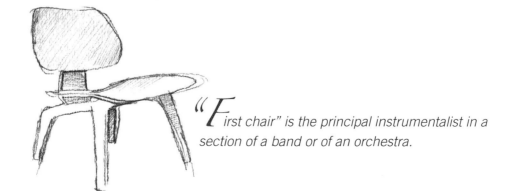

"First chair" is the principal instrumentalist in a section of a band or of an orchestra.

Mandarin Orange Salad with Pecan Croutons

Serves 8

Pecan Croutons
1/2 cup sugar
21/2 tablespoons water
1/2 teaspoon vanilla extract
1 cup pecans, chopped

Salad
1/3 cup olive oil
2 tablespoons red wine vinegar
11/2 teaspoons fresh orange juice
1/2 teaspoon orange zest
1/4 teaspoon poppy seeds
1/8 teaspoon pepper
8 cups mixed salad greens
1 (11-ounce) can mandarin oranges, drained
1 bunch green onions, sliced

To prepare the pecan croutons, mix the sugar, water and vanilla in a saucepan. Bring to a boil and reduce the heat to low. Cook for 5 minutes, stirring occasionally. Stir in the pecans. Spread on a baking sheet to cool. Break apart into pecan croutons.

To prepare the salad, combine the olive oil, vinegar, orange juice, orange zest, poppy seeds and pepper in a jar with a tight-fitting lid. Secure the lid and shake well. Combine the salad greens, oranges and green onions in a bowl and mix well. Add the vinaigrette and toss to coat. Sprinkle with the pecan croutons.

Kathleen Wren Gilliam

Pineapple Salad

Serves 8

1 (3-ounce) package lemon gelatin
1 cup water
1/2 cup sour cream
1/4 cup mayonnaise

1 (13-ounce) can crushed pineapple
1/2 cup (2 ounces) shredded sharp
    Cheddar cheese

Heat the gelatin and water in a medium saucepan until the gelatin dissolves, stirring constantly. Beat in the sour cream and mayonnaise. Stir in the undrained pineapple. Chill until partially set. Fold in the cheese. Pour into a 4-cup mold. Chill until set.

Kathy Johnson Riley

Potato Salad

Serves 6 to 8

6 red potatoes, scrubbed
1/2 cup Italian salad dressing
3 green onions with tops, chopped
1 teaspoon salt
1/2 teaspoon celery salt
1/2 teaspoon seasoned salt
1/4 teaspoon pepper

1 teaspoon dill weed
2 hard-cooked eggs, chopped
11/2 tablespoons mayonnaise
2 teaspoons mustard
Parsley, olives, dill pickles, and so forth
    for garnish

Boil the unpeeled potatoes in a saucepan until fork-tender. Drain and place in a medium bowl. Drizzle the very warm potatoes with the salad dressing. Add the green onions. Cut the potatoes into slices when cool enough to handle. Sprinkle with a mixture of the salt, celery salt, seasoned salt, pepper and dill weed. Add the eggs. Mix the mayonnaise and mustard together. Add to the potato mixture and toss lightly. Garnish with parsley, olives, dill pickles and so forth

Note: It is important to add the salad dressing to very warm potatoes
because the flavor absorbs better than when cool.

Hilda Hughes Church, Dothan, Alabama

South-of-the-Border Salad

Serves 8 to 10

Cilantro Salad Dressing
1/2 cup sour cream
1/2 cup extra-virgin olive oil
1/2 cup lime juice
1/3 cup chopped fresh cilantro
1/2 teaspoon salt
1/2 teaspoon pepper

Salad
2 bunches romaine lettuce, torn into pieces
1 (15-ounce) can black beans, drained and rinsed
1 small purple onion, chopped
1 (8-ounce) package shredded Mexican four-cheese blend
1 (8-ounce) can whole kernel corn, drained
1 (3-ounce) can sliced black olives
1 cup crushed tortilla chips

To prepare the salad dressing, process the sour cream, olive oil, lime juice, cilantro, salt and pepper in a blender until smooth.

To prepare the salad, place the lettuce in a large salad bowl. Add the beans, onion, cheese, corn, olives and tortilla chips. Pour the salad dressing over the salad just before serving and toss gently.

Millie Peacock Patrick

Panzanella

Serves 12

Garlic Vinaigrette
3 tablespoons white wine vinegar
1/2 cup good-quality olive oil
1 teaspoon minced garlic
1/2 teaspoon Dijon mustard
1/2 teaspoon kosher salt
1/4 teaspoon freshly ground pepper

Salad
1 baguette French bread
3 tablespoons (or more) good-quality olive oil
Dash of kosher salt
3 Roma tomatoes, cut into wedges or thick slices
1 pint cherry or pear tomatoes, cut into halves
1 hothouse cucumber, seeded and sliced 1/2 inch thick
1 small red bell pepper, cut into 1-inch cubes
1 small orange bell pepper, cut into 1-inch cubes
1 small yellow bell pepper, cut into 1-inch cubes
1/2 red onion, cut into 1-inch pieces
20 fresh basil leaves, coarsely chopped
1/4 cup capers, drained
1 cup crumbled feta cheese
Salt and pepper to taste

To prepare the vinaigrette, whisk the vinegar, olive oil, garlic, Dijon mustard, kosher salt and pepper in a bowl until blended.

To prepare the salad, brush the bread with the olive oil and sprinkle with kosher salt. Cut into 1-inch cubes. Place on a stove-top grill. Grill for 10 minutes on each side or until brown. Combine the tomatoes, cucumber, bell peppers, onion, basil, capers and cheese in a large salad bowl. Add enough of the vinaigrette to moisten and toss to coat. Season generously with salt and pepper. Drizzle the bread with the remaining vinaigrette or some additional olive oil and add to the salad. Let stand for 30 minutes for the flavors to blend before serving.

Note: If you do not have a stove-top grill, heat the olive oil in a large sauté pan.
Add the bread cubes and salt. Cook over low to medium heat for 10 minutes or until brown,
turning frequently and adding additional olive oil if needed.

Cindy Lesley Alexander

Tomato and Mozzarella Stacks

Serves 1 or 2

2 tablespoons balsamic vinegar	10 to 12 green olives, thinly sliced
2 tablespoons olive oil	1/2 cup (2 ounces) shredded mozzarella
1 large summer tomato, cut into	cheese, or 3 small slices mozzarella
1/2-inch slices	cheese
Salt and pepper to taste	

Blend the vinegar and olive oil in a bowl. Arrange 1 tomato slice on a baking sheet and drizzle with 1 tablespoon of the vinegar mixture. Season with salt and pepper. Layer with 5 or 6 olive slices and sprinkle with some of the cheese. Repeat the process twice. Bake at 350 degrees for 5 minutes. Serve immediately.

Betty Turner Corn

My grandmother Mimi is the central hub of my family. Being the mother of a family of four daughters, Mimi has always been the head of what I'm sure feels like an extremely matriarchal society to my grandfather, Pop. In exchange for her good faith, God gave Mimi a rare knack for music. She has perfect pitch and plays the organ beautifully. Although Mimi has mostly lost her ability to play, she will never lose her love for music. I know this because I was fortunate enough to spend last Christmas supper with Mimi, Pop, and other members of my family. As we took our seats around the supper table to celebrate "Jesus' birthday," Mimi told a brief familial history of the table and chairs and of the china on which we were eating. By divine intervention, Pop broke Christmas protocol and asked Mimi to say the blessing. Without hesitation, she broke into a hymn for our blessing,

HE IS LORD, HE IS LORD
HE HAS RISEN FROM THE DEAD
AND HE IS MY LORD
EVERY KNEE SHALL BOW
AND EVERY TONGUE CONFESS
THAT JESUS CHRIST IS LORD.

Everyone was speechless. Strong circles are formed by human bonds around the structure of a family's dining table, a symbol of unity under love and common purpose. We all felt unified by this blessing.

— *Mitchell Jarrett*, Athens, Georgia

Cotton Gin Pasta

Serves 8 to 10

1 (16-ounce) package acini di pepe or ditalini
1¹/2 cups sour cream
1¹/2 cups mayonnaise
1 cucumber, peeled, seeded and chopped
3 (or more) green onions, chopped
1 tablespoon (or more) chopped fresh dill weed
Salt and pepper to taste

Cook the pasta in a large saucepan using the package directions; drain well. Mix 1 cup of the sour cream and 1 cup of the mayonnaise in a bowl until blended. Add to the pasta and mix well. Add the cucumber, green onions, dill weed, salt and pepper and mix well. Chill for 1 to 2 hours. Add the remaining 1/2 cup sour cream and 1/2 cup mayonnaise and mix well. Sprinkle with salt and pepper.

Libby McGill Hattaway, Blakely, Georgia

Muffuletta Orzo Salad

Serves 6

1¹/2 teaspoons minced garlic
2 tablespoons red wine vinegar
2 tablespoons extra-virgin olive oil
2 tablespoons green olive juice
2 teaspoons lemon juice
1/2 teaspoon red chile flakes
1/2 teaspoon black pepper
1/4 cup black olives
1/4 cup pimento-stuffed green olives
1/4 cup marinated artichoke hearts
1/4 cup roasted red bell peppers
1 cup cooked orzo
1/4 cup crumbled feta cheese
1/4 cup chopped Roma tomatoes

Pulse the garlic, vinegar, olive oil, olive juice, lemon juice, red chile flakes, black pepper, black olives, green olives, artichokes and bell peppers in a food processor until well chopped but not puréed. Spoon into a bowl. Chill for 2 hours or longer. Add the orzo and cheese and mix well. Spoon into a serving bowl. Top with the tomatoes and serve.

Michelle Williams Hudson

Orzo Pasta Salad

Serves 6 to 8

A superb addition to any picnic basket.

Honey Lemon Vinaigrette
1/2 cup red wine vinegar
1 tablespoon honey
1 teaspoon lemon juice
1/2 teaspoon salt
1/8 teaspoon pepper
3/4 cup olive oil

Salad
16 ounces orzo, cooked and drained
1/2 cup garbanzo beans, drained and rinsed
1/4 cup chopped red onion
1/2 cup chopped tomato
1/2 cup freshly chopped basil
4 ounces capers, drained
1/2 cup chopped seeded cucumber
3 tablespoons crumbled feta cheese

To prepare the vinaigrette, process the vinegar, honey, lemon juice, salt and pepper in a blender until blended. Adjust the seasonings to taste. Add the olive oil gradually, processing constantly. Pour into a small container.

To prepare the salad, combine the pasta, beans, onion, tomato, basil, capers, cucumber and cheese in a bowl and toss to mix. Add the vinaigrette and toss to coat. Serve at room temperature.

Charlotte Lee Bowman

Early rocking chairs were known as "carpet cutters" because of the damage done to carpets by repeated rocking in the same place.

Savannah Pasta Salad

Serves 14 to 16

1 (16-ounce) package elbow macaroni	3 Roma tomatoes, seeded and chopped
1 (8-ounce) jar sliced green olives	2 cups good-quality mayonnaise
1 pound sharp Cheddar cheese, crumbled	2 teaspoons garlic salt
1 Vidalia onion, finely chopped	1 teaspoon freshly ground pepper

Cook the pasta in a saucepan using the package directions; drain. Let stand until cool. Drain 2 tablespoons of the brine from the olives and discard. Combine the pasta, olives with remaining brine, cheese, onion, tomatoes, mayonnaise, garlic salt and pepper in a large serving bowl and mix well. Adjust the seasonings to taste.

Resa Pate Carter

Confetti Rice Salad

Serves 10 to 12

4 cups cooked rice	15 cherry tomatoes, cut into halves
1 (8-ounce) can mixed vegetables, drained	2 tablespoons finely chopped green bell pepper
1 (7-ounce) can whole kernel corn with sweet peppers	2 tablespoons chopped green onions
1 cup mayonnaise	Dash of garlic powder
1/4 cup vinegar	Salt and pepper to taste
1/4 cup vegetable oil	Lettuce leaves for garnish
1/2 cup chopped celery	

Combine the rice, mixed vegetables, corn, mayonnaise, vinegar, oil, celery, tomatoes, bell pepper, green onions, garlic powder, salt and pepper in a large bowl and mix well. Chill, covered, until serving time. To serve, line a large serving bowl with lettuce. Spoon the rice mixture into the prepared bowl.

Julie Smith Alexander

Rice and Artichoke Salad

Serves 8

Shrimp or chicken can easily be added to this recipe.

1 (8-ounce) package chicken Rice-A-Roni
1 (12-ounce) jar marinated artichoke hearts
2 green onions, sliced

1/2 green bell pepper, chopped
1/3 cup mayonnaise
1/2 teaspoon curry powder

Cook the Rice-A-Roni in a saucepan using the package directions. Remove from the heat to cool. Drain the artichoke hearts, reserving 1/3 to 1/2 cup of the marinade. Cut the artichoke hearts into small pieces with kitchen shears. Combine the Rice-A-Roni, artichoke heart pieces, green onions and bell pepper in a medium bowl and mix well. Mix the mayonnaise and curry powder in a small bowl. Add enough of the reserved marinade to make a thin paste. Add to the rice mixture and toss to mix. Chill until serving time.

Sandy Tally Coolik

Spinach and Rice Salad

Serves 4

1/2 cup Italian salad dressing
2 tablespoons soy sauce
1/2 teaspoon sugar
1 cup cooked white rice

2 cups fresh spinach, cut into thin strips
1/2 cup chopped celery
1/2 cup chopped green onions
1/2 to 1 cup crumbled cooked bacon

Combine the salad dressing, soy sauce and sugar in a salad bowl and mix well with the rice. Add the spinach, celery and green onions and toss to mix. Sprinkle with the bacon.

Jennifer Gillespie Daniel

West Indies Salad

Serves 10 to 12

1 onion, chopped
Salt and pepper to taste
2 or 3 ribs celery, chopped
1 pound lump crab meat

1/2 cup vegetable oil
1/2 cup apple cider vinegar
6 tablespoons ice water

Layer the onion, salt, pepper, celery and crab meat in a salad bowl. Mix the oil, vinegar and water in a bowl. Pour over the layers. Marinate, covered, in the refrigerator for 2 to 12 hours.

Note: Serve on a bed of lettuce or with melba rounds as an appetizer.

Hilda Hughes Church, Dothan, Alabama

Chicken Salad

Serves 10

1 bunch celery
1 sweet onion
6 boneless skinless chicken breasts
Salt and pepper to taste
1 cup pecan halves

2 tablespoons lemon juice, or more to taste
1 teaspoon cayenne pepper
1/2 teaspoon salt
1/2 teaspoon pepper
1 cup mayonnaise, or to taste

Reserve 6 ribs of the celery and chop. Finely chop enough of the onion to yield 1 tablespoon. Cut the remaining onion into quarters. Place the chicken, remaining celery ribs, onion quarters and salt and pepper to taste in a saucepan. Cover with water and bring to a boil. Cook for 40 minutes or until the chicken is cooked through. Spread the pecans on a baking sheet. Bake at 350 degrees for 15 minutes or until toasted. Chop the toasted pecans.

Drain the chicken, discarding the liquid and vegetables. Shred the chicken and cut into small pieces. Combine the chicken, reserved chopped celery, finely chopped onion, 2 tablespoons lemon juice, the cayenne pepper, 1/2 teaspoon salt, 1/2 teaspoon pepper and the pecans in a bowl and mix well. Add enough of the mayonnaise to bind. Adjust the lemon juice and seasonings to taste.

Mary Lynn Pugh Grubb

Curried Chicken Salad

Serves 6

4 or 5 boneless chicken breasts	Dash of pepper
1 cup chicken broth	2 splashes of lemon juice
1 cup mayonnaise	1/2 cantaloupe, cut into bite-size pieces
Curry powder to taste	1 cup green grapes, cut into halves

Place the chicken and broth in a saucepan. Add enough water to cover the chicken and bring to a boil. Cook until the chicken is cooked through. Remove from the heat to cool. Mix the mayonnaise, curry powder, pepper and lemon juice in a large bowl. Cut the chicken into bite-size pieces. Add to the curry powder mixture and mix well. Fold in the cantaloupe and grape halves.

Note: You should add enough curry powder to turn the mayonnaise mixture light yellow. If a stronger curry flavor is desired, add up to 2 tablespoons. Also, additional grape halves and cantaloupe pieces can be added as filler.

Olivia Cheves Blanchard

Zesty Salad Sandwich

Serves 4 to 6

1 round loaf fresh sourdough bread	1/3 pound Black Forest deli ham,
1/4 cup red wine vinegar	very thinly sliced
4 slices Gouda cheese	1 1/2 cups shredded iceberg lettuce
5 slices Genoa salami	2 tomatoes, peeled and chopped
1/3 pound deli smoked turkey,	1/3 cup red wine vinegar and olive oil
very thinly sliced	salad dressing

Cut the bread into halves lengthwise and hollow out the bread until about one-half shell remains. Drizzle 2 tablespoons vinegar into each half. Layer the cheese and salami on the bottom half. Pile the turkey and ham on top. Toss the lettuce and tomatoes with the salad dressing in a bowl. Place on top of the ham. Replace the top half of the bread so the halves touch each other. Wrap in plastic wrap. Chill for 4 to 10 hours. Cut into wedges, placing a wooden pick in each wedge to hold together.

Anne Hayes Drinkard Pearce

Grilled Chicken on French Bread

Serves 4

1 loaf French bread	1/2 green bell pepper, thinly sliced
1 tablespoon steak rub	1/4 red onion, thinly sliced
2 tablespoons extra-virgin olive oil	1 tablespoon extra-virgin olive oil
2 boneless chicken breasts	1 tablespoon balsamic vinegar
1/2 red bell pepper, thinly sliced	4 ounces feta cheese, crumbled

Cut the bread into halves lengthwise and place on a baking sheet. Bake at 350 degrees until toasted. Mix the steak rub with 2 tablespoons olive oil in a bowl. Spread on the chicken and place on a grill rack. Grill until cooked through. Let stand until cool. Cut into bite-size pieces. Sauté the bell peppers and onion in 1 tablespoon olive oil and the vinegar in a skillet over high heat. Spread the cheese on the cut sides of the bread. Layer the sautéed vegetables and chicken on the bottom half of the bread. Top with the remaining half of the bread. Cut into four pieces.

Meghan Kennedy Rumer

Sandwich Delight

Serves 8

Sandwich Sauce
1 1/2 cups mayonnaise
1/2 cup sour cream
3 to 4 tablespoons chili sauce
1 tablespoon chives
1 tablespoon lime juice
Dash of Tabasco sauce
Salt and pepper to taste

Sandwiches
8 slices Canadian bacon
8 slices Muenster cheese
16 to 24 slices cooked chicken or
  turkey breast
8 to 16 lettuce leaves
8 to 16 slices tomato
16 slices bacon, crisp-cooked and drained
8 slices Holland rusk or your favorite
  sandwich bread
Black caviar for garnish
Chopped chives for garnish

To prepare the sauce, combine the mayonnaise, sour cream, chili sauce, chives, lime juice, Tabasco sauce, salt and pepper in a bowl and mix well. Chill, covered, for 2 hours. The sauce may be stored in the refrigerator for up to 4 days.

To prepare the sandwiches, layer 1 slice of the Canadian bacon, 1 slice of the cheese, 2 or 3 slices of the chicken, 1 or 2 lettuce leaves, 1 or 2 tomato slices and 2 crisp bacon slices on top of each slice of rusk. Drizzle with the sauce. Garnish with caviar and chives and serve immediately.

Mary Dana Huntley Knight

Sunday Night Sandwich

Serves 6

An updated version of the original recipe by Calvin DesPortes
in A Southern Collection.

1 pound white crab meat
2 to 3 tablespoons (or more) mayonnaise
Juice of 1/2 lemon, or more to taste
1/2 teaspoon dry mustard
Dash of Tabasco sauce
Dash of Worcestershire sauce

6 slices bread, lightly toasted
1/2 cup (2 ounces) shredded sharp
   Cheddar cheese
1 tomato, sliced
6 slices bacon, crisp-cooked and
   cut into halves

Combine the crab meat, mayonnaise, lemon juice, dry mustard, Tabasco sauce and Worcestershire sauce in a small bowl and mix well. Adjust the seasonings to taste and add additional mayonnaise and lemon juice if needed. Spread thickly over the toasted bread. Cover each with the cheese, a slice of tomato and two half-slices of bacon. Place on a baking sheet. Broil until the cheese melts.

Betty Turner Corn

Pimento Cheese

Serves 12 to 14

3 cups (12 ounces) shredded good-quality
   sharp Cheddar cheese
1 small jar chopped pimento, drained
1/2 teaspoon dry mustard
3 shakes of onion salt
3 shakes of garlic powder

Dash of salt
Dash of sugar
Red pepper to taste
1 teaspoon Worcestershire sauce
3 or 4 drops of Tabasco sauce
Mayonnaise

Combine the cheese, pimento, dry mustard, onion salt, garlic powder, salt, sugar, red pepper, Worcestershire sauce and Tabasco sauce in a bowl and mix well. Stir in enough mayonnaise to bind. Chill, covered, until serving time.

Tiffany Kitchens Wilson

Meme's Tomato Sandwich

Makes 1 sandwich

For a simply delicious variation, add slices of crisp-cooked bacon,
fresh dill weed, basil or tarragon, and homemade mayonnaise.

2 slices white bread
1 teaspoon Homemade Basil Mayonnaise (see Note)
4 thin slices tomato
Salt to taste

Spread each slice of bread with the mayonnaise. Layer the tomato on one slice of the bread and sprinkle with salt. Top with the remaining bread slice and serve.

Note: To make Homemade Basil Mayonnaise, process 2 tablespoons vinegar, 2 eggs, 2 tablespoons lemon juice, 1 teaspoon salt, 1/2 teaspoon dry mustard and 1/4 cup vegetable oil in a food processor or blender until blended. Drip 2 1/4 cups vegetable oil into the mixture gradually, processing constantly until emulsified. Stir in 2 tablespoons chopped basil. If you are concerned about using raw eggs, use eggs pasteurized in their shells, which are sold at some specialty food stores.

Christopher Stevenson Woodruff

My grandfather, Barnett Woodruff, often recounts the story of his honeymoon to me on our visits to 3 Lakes Lodge. Newly married, Papa and Meme spent their first nights of wedded bliss at the cabin on 3 Lakes. It was the first evening and Meme, the young new bride, offered to make her husband their first meal together. Not yet familiar with the kitchen, Meme made her finest attempt at what she knew best—Tomato Sandwiches. Papa always used to say, "For three days, we sat on the porch and ate those tomato sandwiches…and you know, those were the best sandwiches I ever had."

— Christopher Stevenson Woodruff

From Lawnchairs to Ladderbacks

Vegetables & Sides

"Riverside" was owned by my grandfather, Arthur Bussey, and it was the Bussey summer home

from 1908 to 1918. My mother, Sara Bussey Bickerstaff, told many wonderful tales about those summers.

In "Chidlhood Memories of Riverside," she wrote, "Eleanor and I climbed one tree by the house.

We would get 'city girls' up in this tree and leave them to get down as best they could.

We would then go pull up a chair on the verandah and watch as they struggled. We always softened and

got them down foot by foot. Commanding General Tom Tarpley called it our Bloomer Tree."

Columbus is proud to be home to Fort Benning, the nation's largest infantry base.

Riverside is now the home of the presiding commanding general.

—Sally Bickerstaff Hatcher

From Lawnchairs to Ladderbacks

Vegetables & Sides

Green Beans with Walnut Dill Dressing

Serves 6

A wonderful complement to fish. This dish is best served at room temperature or slightly warmed.

1 cup walnuts	1/2 cup fresh dill weed, trimmed
Salt to taste	1/4 cup flat-leaf parsley, trimmed
2 quarts water	6 scallions, coarsely chopped
1 1/2 pounds green beans, trimmed and cut into 2- to 3-inch pieces	1/3 cup olive oil
	Salt and pepper to taste
3 tablespoons lemon juice	

Place the walnuts in a single layer on a baking sheet. Roast at 350 degrees for 5 minutes. Remove from the oven to cool completely. Bring lightly salted water to a boil in a saucepan. Add the beans. Cook for 5 to 7 minutes or until tender-crisp. Drain and plunge immediately into ice water to stop the cooking process. Drain well and place in a large bowl. Blend the lemon juice, dill weed, parsley, scallions, walnuts and olive oil in a blender or food processor for 30 seconds or until the mixture is combined but still has texture. Pour over the beans and toss to coat. Sprinkle with salt and pepper.

Note: Feta cheese crumbles to taste can be added.

Mary Lynn Pugh Grubb

Braised Green Beans

Serves 6

2 tablespoons olive oil	3/4 cup low-sodium chicken broth
1 shallot, minced	Salt and pepper to taste
1 pound green beans, trimmed	

Heat the olive oil in a skillet. Add the shallot. Sauté for 5 minutes or until golden brown. Add the beans and broth. Cover and reduce the heat. Simmer for 15 minutes. Sprinkle with salt and pepper.

Clara Turner Middlebrooks

Divine Green Bean Casserole

Serves 6

3/4 cup finely chopped celery
3 tablespoons finely chopped onion
1 1/2 teaspoons olive oil
1/2 cup sour cream
1 (10-ounce) can cream of celery soup
1 (11-ounce) can Shoe Peg corn, drained

2 (14-ounce) cans French green beans, drained
3/4 cup (3 ounces) shredded sharp Cheddar cheese
2 cups butter crackers, crushed
1/4 cup (1/2 stick) butter, or to taste

Sauté the celery and onion in the olive oil in a skillet until tender. Add the sour cream and mix well. Stir in the soup, corn, beans and cheese. Place in a greased 9×13-inch baking dish. Sprinkle with the cracker crumbs. Dot with the butter. Bake, uncovered, at 350 degrees for 45 to 60 minutes or until bubbly.

Dradyn Coolik Hinson

Baked Beans

Serves 4

2 garlic cloves, minced
3 onions, thinly sliced
1/4 cup vegetable oil or bacon drippings
1 (14-ounce) can baked beans
1 (14-ounce) can red kidney beans, drained
1 (14-ounce) can small green lima beans, drained

1/2 cup packed brown sugar
1/4 cup vinegar
1/2 cup ketchup
1 teaspoon prepared or dry mustard
1 teaspoon salt
1 jigger of brandy

Cook the garlic and onions in the oil in a skillet until translucent. Add the baked beans, kidney beans, lima beans, brown sugar, vinegar, ketchup, mustard and salt and mix well. Pour into a 2-quart baking dish or bean pot. Chill in the refrigerator. Stir well before baking. Bake at 350 degrees for 1 to 1 1/4 hours or until bubbly. Stir in the brandy just before serving.

Mary Dana Huntley Knight

Broccoli Casserole

Serves 12

3 (10-ounce) packages frozen broccoli or
fresh equivalent
6 tablespoons butter
6 tablespoons all-purpose flour
16 ounces cottage cheese

6 eggs, beaten
1 pound sharp Cheddar cheese, shredded
Dash of red pepper
Salt and black pepper to taste

Cook the broccoli using the package directions or steam fresh broccoli until tender-crisp. Melt the butter in a saucepan. Stir in the flour. Cook for several minutes, stirring constantly. Add the broccoli, cottage cheese and eggs. Reserve a portion of the cheese for topping. Stir the remaining cheese, red pepper, salt and black pepper into the broccoli mixture. Spoon into a large baking dish and sprinkle with the reserved cheese. Place in a larger baking dish and add enough water to come halfway up the side of the smaller dish. Bake at 350 degrees for 45 minutes.

Note: This casserole can be frozen before baking.

Marquin Conklin Barrett, Augusta, Georgia

Blue Cheese Brussels Sprouts

Serves 4

Even the children will ask for a second helping.

1 pound brussels sprouts, ends trimmed
and yellow leaves removed
1/4 cup (1/2 stick) butter, sliced
Kosher salt to taste
Freshly cracked pepper to taste

Juice of 1/2 lemon
1/4 cup crumbled blue cheese
3 or 4 slices bacon, crisp-cooked
and crumbled

Place the brussels sprouts in a baking dish or Dutch oven with a lid. Top with the butter. Add kosher salt, pepper and lemon juice. Bake, covered, at 350 degrees for 25 minutes or until tender-crisp, stirring occasionally. Sprinkle with the cheese and bacon. Serve immediately.

Millie Peacock Patrick

Carrot Soufflé

Serves 6

1 large bunch carrots, peeled
2 tablespoons butter
1 tablespoon all-purpose flour
1 cup milk
3 or 4 tablespoons sugar
2 eggs

Cook the carrots in boiling water in a saucepan until tender. Drain and mash the carrots. Melt the butter in a saucepan. Stir in the flour. Add the milk. Cook until thickened, stirring constantly. Add with the sugar to the carrots and mix well. Beat the eggs in a bowl until light. Stir into the carrot mixture. Spoon into an 8×8-inch baking dish. Bake at 325 degrees for 1 hour or until firm in the center.

Helen Jackson Burgin

Cool Carrots

Serves 8 to 10

1 bunch carrots, peeled
Salt to taste
1 large onion, thinly sliced and cut into halves
1 (10-ounce) can cream of tomato soup
3/4 cup vinegar
1/2 cup vegetable oil
1 cup sugar
1 teaspoon mustard
1 teaspoon Worcestershire sauce

Boil the carrots in salted water in a saucepan until tender. Drain and cool. Cut the carrots into 1/2-inch slices. Alternate layers of the carrots and onion in a large bowl. Bring the soup, vinegar, oil, sugar, mustard and Worcestershire sauce to a boil in a saucepan, stirring constantly. Pour over the layers. Chill for 8 to 10 hours before serving.

Jennifer Ellington Walker

Claudia's Summertime Corn

Serves 6 to 8

5 ears of white Silver Queen corn, shucked
Salt to taste
1/2 cup chopped red onion
1/2 cup chopped summer tomatoes
3 tablespoons apple cider vinegar

3 tablespoons good-quality olive oil
1/2 teaspoon kosher salt
1/2 teaspoon freshly ground pepper
1/2 cup fresh basil leaves

Boil the corn in salted water in a large stockpot for 5 minutes or until the starchiness is gone. Do not overcook. Drain and plunge immediately into ice water to stop the cooking process. Let stand until cool. Cut the kernels from the cobs into a large bowl. Add the onion, tomatoes, vinegar, olive oil, kosher salt and pepper and toss to mix. Stir in the basil just before serving.

Claudia Sessions Garrard

Baked Corn

Serves 6 to 8

1 (16-ounce) package frozen Shoe Peg corn
1 cup skim milk
2 tablespoons all-purpose flour
3 tablespoons sugar

1/2 teaspoon salt
2 tablespoons butter, melted
2 teaspoons pepper
2 eggs

Pulse the frozen corn, milk, flour, sugar, salt, butter, pepper and eggs in a food processor several times. Do not over-process. Pour into a greased 9×13-inch glass baking dish. Bake at 350 degrees for 40 to 45 minutes or until brown on top.

Note: Do not thaw the corn.

Dori Sponcler Jones

Curried Cauliflower

Serves 6

1 head cauliflower
1/2 teaspoon salt
1 (10-ounce) can cream of chicken soup
1/3 cup mayonnaise
2 tablespoons margarine, melted

1 teaspoon curry powder
1 cup (4 ounces) shredded
  Cheddar cheese
1/4 cup dry bread crumbs

Boil the cauliflower with the salt in water in a saucepan until tender. Drain and cut into florets. Combine the cauliflower, soup, mayonnaise, margarine, curry powder and cheese in a bowl and mix well. Spoon into a lightly greased 8×8-inch glass baking dish. Sprinkle with the bread crumbs. Bake at 350 degrees for 30 minutes.

Sandy Tally Coolik

Eggplant Patrice

Serves 6

1 small eggplant
2 tomatoes, sliced
1 onion, chopped
1 green bell pepper, chopped

Salt, garlic salt and pepper to taste
1 1/2 cups (6 ounces) shredded sharp
  Cheddar cheese

Cut the unpeeled eggplant into slices 1/4 inch thick. Parboil in water in a saucepan until partially tender. Layer the eggplant, tomatoes, onion, bell pepper, salt, garlic salt, pepper and cheese one-half at a time in a baking dish. Bake, covered, at 400 degrees until the mixture steams. Uncover and reduce the oven temperature to 350 degrees. Bake for 30 to 45 minutes or until the eggplant is tender and the sauce is thick and golden brown.

Margaret Glenn Zollo

Parmesan-Roasted Fennel

Serves 4 to 6

2 or 3 fennel bulbs
Olive oil for drizzling
Kosher salt to taste
Freshly ground black pepper to taste

Freshly ground white pepper to taste
1/2 cup (2 ounces) freshly grated
Parmesan cheese

Remove and discard the tough outer leaves of the fennel bulbs. Remove and coarsely chop 2 teaspoons of the fronds and reserve for garnish. Cut the bulb crosswise into 1/2-inch slices. Arrange the sliced fennel bulb in a slightly overlapping single layer in a 9×13-inch baking dish. Drizzle with olive oil. Sprinkle generously with kosher salt, black pepper and white pepper. Sprinkle generously with the cheese. Bake at 375 degrees for 45 minutes or until golden brown. Garnish with the reserved fronds.

Teresa Carswell Howard

Portobello Mushrooms in Garlic Wine Sauce

Serves 4

Excellent served over steak.

8 ounces whole portobello mushrooms
2 tablespoons butter
1/4 cup chopped red onion

4 garlic cloves, crushed
1/4 cup marsala
1/2 teaspoon seasoned salt

Rinse the mushrooms and pat dry, removing the stems if desired. Heat a sauté pan over medium-high heat for 2 minutes. Place the butter, onion and garlic in the hot pan. Sauté for 2 minutes or until brown. Stir in the mushrooms, wine and seasoned salt. Reduce the heat to medium. Cook, covered, for 5 to 7 minutes, stirring occasionally.

Wendy Ryan Gay

Curried Baked Onions

Serves 6 to 8

A wonderful accompaniment to beef roast.

3 large onions, sliced	Brown sugar for sprinkling
Butter for dotting	Curry powder for sprinkling

Cut the onions into slices 1/2 inch thick. Place in a baking dish. Dot each slice with butter and sprinkle with brown sugar and curry powder. Bake at 350 degrees for 15 to 20 minutes or until tender.

Sue Marie Thompson Turner

Parmesan Vidalia Onions

Serves 6 to 8

5 large Vidalia onions, sliced	1 sleeve butter crackers, crushed
2 tablespoons butter	1 cup (4 ounces) freshly grated
Salt and pepper to taste	Parmesan cheese

Sauté the onions in the butter in a skillet until soft and golden brown. Layer the onions, salt, pepper, cracker crumbs and cheese one-third at a time in an 8×8-inch baking pan. Bake at 350 degrees for 25 to 30 minutes or until bubbly. Broil until the top is brown.

Michelle Williams Hudson

"Worry is like a rocking chair—it gives you something to do but it doesn't get you anywhere."

— Glenn Turner

Okra Creole

Serves 4 to 6

Many locals are proud to grow okra in their summer gardens, and this recipe offers a twist to the South's popular fried version.

1 cup chopped onion	1 tablespoon ketchup
2 garlic cloves, chopped	1/2 teaspoon vinegar
1/4 cup olive oil	2 tablespoons Creole seasoning
1 pound fresh or frozen okra, cut into	1/2 teaspoon pepper
1-inch pieces	1/2 teaspoon Worcestershire sauce
1 (14-ounce) can chicken broth	

Sauté the onion and garlic in the olive oil in a skillet until tender. Add the okra and sauté for 1 minute. Add the broth, ketchup, vinegar, Creole seasoning, pepper and Worcestershire sauce and mix well. Cook, covered, over medium heat for 30 minutes. Serve warm.

Edie Pendleton Evans

Rennie's Sautéed Okra

Serves 4

8 ounces fresh or frozen okra	1/2 teaspoon garlic powder
5 to 6 tablespoons olive oil	2 or 3 sun-dried tomatoes, drained and
Peppercorns to taste	coarsely chopped (optional)

Cut the okra lengthwise, keeping the crown. Pour enough of the olive oil into a sauté pan to coat the bottom. Heat the olive oil and add peppercorns. Sauté for 2 to 3 minutes to flavor the olive oil. Add the okra with the seed side down. Sprinkle with the garlic powder. Cook over medium heat for 5 minutes or until light brown. Add the tomatoes. Cook for 2 minutes. Remove to paper towels to drain.

Note: Brussels sprouts can be used instead of the okra.

Walker Reynolds (Rennie) Bickerstaff

Au Gratin Potatoes

Serves 10 to 12

8 new or red potatoes, scrubbed	2 cups (8 ounces) shredded sharp
Salt to taste	Cheddar cheese
1 large onion	Pepper to taste
8 tablespoons (1 stick) butter	2 to 3 tablespoons chopped parsley
6 tablespoons all-purpose flour	Paprika for garnish
3 cups milk	

Boil the unpeeled whole potatoes in salted water in a saucepan for 20 minutes or until tender. Drain and set aside to cool. Peel the potatoes and cut into cubes. Sauté the onion in 2 tablespoons of the butter in a skillet until translucent. Melt the remaining butter in a saucepan. Stir in the flour. Add the milk. Cook until thickened, stirring constantly. Stir in the cheese. Add the onion, salt, pepper and parsley and mix well. Add the potatoes and mix well. Spoon into a baking dish. Garnish with paprika. Bake at 300 degrees for 30 minutes or until bubbly.

Dell McMath Turner

Blue Cheese Mashed Potatoes

Serves 4 to 6

If you don't like blue cheese, goat cheese is also an excellent addition to traditional mashed potatoes.

4 or 5 large potatoes, peeled	1/2 cup sour cream
1/2 to 1 cup whipping cream	1/2 cup mayonnaise
1/2 cup milk	Salt and pepper to taste
1/4 cup (1/2 stick) butter	1/4 cup crumbled blue cheese

Place the potatoes in a saucepan and cover with cold water. Bring to a boil. Boil for 20 minutes or until tender; drain. Heat the cream, milk and butter in a saucepan until the butter melts. Combine the potatoes and cream mixture in a mixing bowl and beat well. Add the sour cream and mayonnaise and mix well. Add salt and pepper. Beat in enough of the cheese at medium speed to achieve the desired consistency.

Lisa McMullen Allen

Gratin Dauphinoise

Serves 6 to 8

Butter for greasing
1 garlic clove, cut into halves
1 1/2 cups milk
Salt and pepper to taste

Nutmeg to taste
2 pounds potatoes, sliced (about 5)
1/2 cup cream
4 ounces Gruyère cheese, shredded

Grease a baking dish with butter and rub with the garlic. Bring the milk, salt, pepper and nutmeg to a boil in a saucepan. Add the potatoes a handful at a time so the milk mixture maintains a simmer. Return to a boil and cook for 5 minutes. Pour into the prepared baking dish. Add the cream and cheese. Bake at 375 degrees for 25 to 30 minutes or until bubbly.

Note: To reheat, add a small amount of cream.

Martha King Cunningham

Twice-Baked Potatoes

Serves 8

4 baking potatoes
8 to 10 ounces light sour cream
1/4 cup (1/2 stick) margarine
1 teaspoon paprika
1 teaspoon salt
1 teaspoon pepper

1 tablespoon dried parsley
1/3 cup shredded Cheddar cheese
1/3 cup grated Parmesan cheese or
   crumbled feta cheese
1 bunch green onions, chopped

Scrub the potatoes. Bake at 400 degrees for 1 hour or until tender. Cut the potatoes into halves lengthwise. Scoop out the potato and place in a bowl, reserving the skin shells. Add the sour cream, margarine, paprika, salt, pepper, parsley, Cheddar cheese, Parmesan cheese and green onions to the potatoes and mix well. Spoon into the reserved potato skins. Place on a baking sheet. Bake at 350 degrees for 10 to 15 minutes or until heated through and light golden brown on top.

Note: You can make the potatoes ahead of time and chill or freeze until baking time.

Amelia Alcorn Vaught

Spinach Madeleine

Serves 8

2 (10-ounce) packages frozen
chopped spinach
1/4 cup chopped onion
3 garlic cloves, minced
2 tablespoons butter
1/4 cup all-purpose flour
8 ounces Velveeta cheese, cut into cubes
1/2 cup evaporated milk

1 teaspoon Worcestershire sauce
1 teaspoon salt
1/2 teaspoon black pepper
1/4 teaspoon cayenne pepper, or less
   to taste
1 sleeve butter crackers, crumbled
1/4 cup (1/2 stick) butter, melted

Cook the spinach using the package directions, adding the onion and garlic. Drain, reserving 1/2 cup of the liquid. Melt 2 tablespoons butter in a saucepan. Add the flour. Cook over low heat for 4 to 5 minutes, stirring constantly. Do not brown. Add the reserved liquid. Cook until thickened, stirring constantly. Add the cheese, evaporated milk, Worcestershire sauce, salt, black pepper and cayenne pepper. Cook until the cheese melts, stirring constantly. Add the spinach and mix well. Pour into a 2-quart baking dish. Mix the butter crackers and 1/4 cup butter in a bowl. Sprinkle over the spinach mixture. Bake at 350 degrees until bubbly.

Candice Lamare Wayman

So-Simple Spinach

Serves 4

1/2 garlic clove, minced
2 tablespoons olive oil
1 small slice butter

4 cups fresh spinach
Salt and pepper to taste
1/4 teaspoon nutmeg

Sauté the garlic in the olive oil and butter in a skillet over medium heat for 5 minutes. Reduce the heat to low. Add the spinach. Cook for 3 minutes or until the spinach is barely tender, stirring frequently. Turn off the heat. Sprinkle with salt, pepper and nutmeg. Stir and serve.

Eleanor Glenn Hardegree

Squash Boats

Serves 8

8 squash with stems
1 cup chopped green onions with some tops
4 slices bacon, crisp-cooked and crumbled
1 large tomato, chopped

1 cup (4 ounces) shredded Monterey Jack cheese
Salt and pepper to taste
1 cup bread crumbs
3 tablespoons butter, melted

Place the squash in a saucepan and cover with water. Bring to a boil and reduce the heat. Simmer for 10 minutes or until tender but firm. Drain and cool. Place the squash on a hard surface. Slice off about one-third of the top of each squash to create the boat, leaving the stem intact. Scoop out the center pulp and place in a bowl, reserving the shells. Stir the green onions, bacon, tomato, cheese, salt and pepper into the squash pulp. Spoon into the reserved squash shells. Sprinkle each with the bread crumbs and drizzle with the butter. Place in a baking dish. Bake at 400 degrees for 20 minutes or until the bread crumbs are light brown.

Margaret Bradley McCormick

Yellow Squash with White Wine

Serves 6

Once perfected by Mrs. Laura Ann Phinizy Segrest, this became a favorite recipe of the Colonial Dames.

2 pounds yellow squash, sliced and quartered
1 cup chopped onion
1 teaspoon salt
1 cup sour cream
1/3 cup grated Parmesan cheese

1 1/4 cups cubed sharp Cheddar cheese
1/4 cup vermouth or dry white wine
1/4 cup (1/2 stick) butter
Salt and freshly ground pepper to taste
2 tablespoons butter
8 to 10 saltine crackers, crushed

Place the squash, onion and 1 teaspoon salt in a saucepan. Cover with water and bring to a boil. Boil for 5 minutes or until barely tender; drain. Add the sour cream, Parmesan cheese, Cheddar cheese, wine and 1/4 cup butter and mix well. Add salt and pepper to taste. Pour into a lightly greased 11-inch gratin dish. Melt 2 tablespoons butter in a sauté pan. Add the cracker crumbs. Sauté until light brown. Sprinkle over the squash mixture. Bake at 350 degrees for 20 to 30 minutes or until bubbly.

Margaret Glenn Zollo

Zucchini Casserole

Serves 12

5 eggs
1/2 cup all-purpose flour
1 teaspoon baking powder
1 teaspoon salt
1 teaspoon pepper
6 zucchini, grated
8 to 12 ounces Monterey Jack
cheese, shredded

Beat the eggs in a mixing bowl. Add the flour, baking powder, salt and pepper. Add the zucchini and one-half of the cheese. Spoon into a greased 2-quart round baking dish. Sprinkle with the remaining cheese. Bake at 350 degrees for 45 minutes or until set.

Sandy Tally Coolik

Sweet Potato Casserole

Serves 8 to 10

3 cups mashed canned sweet potatoes
1 cup sugar
1/2 cup (1 stick) butter, melted
2 eggs, beaten
1/3 cup milk
1 teaspoon vanilla extract
1/2 cup packed dark brown sugar
1/4 cup all-purpose flour
1/3 cup butter, melted
1 cup chopped pecans

Combine the sweet potatoes, sugar, 1/2 cup butter, the eggs, milk and vanilla in a bowl and mix until smooth. Spoon into a greased baking dish. Mix the brown sugar, flour, 1/3 cup butter and the pecans in a bowl. Spread over the sweet potato mixture. Bake at 350 degrees for 30 minutes.

Mary Sprouse Boyd

Fried Green Tomatoes with Buttermilk Dressing

Serves 3 to 4

Jamie Keating is the Executive Chef at the River Mill Café in Columbus, Georgia, and is a member of the American Culinary Federation National Culinary Team USA.

Buttermilk Dressing	Green Tomatoes
1/4 cup buttermilk	3 cups canola oil
2 tablespoons mayonnaise	1 cup all-purpose flour
2 tablespoons sugar	1 teaspoon kosher salt
1 tablespoon vinegar	1/4 teaspoon pepper
	2 tomatoes, each cut into 8 slices
	2 eggs, beaten
	3 cups cornflakes, crushed

To prepare the dressing, whisk the buttermilk, mayonnaise, sugar and vinegar in a bowl .

To prepare the tomatoes, heat the canola oil to 325 degrees in a cast-iron skillet. Mix the flour, kosher salt and pepper in a bowl. Dredge the tomato slices in the flour mixture. Coat with the eggs and then dredge in the cornflake crumbs. Fry in the hot oil until golden brown. Serve with the dressing.

Jamie Keating

Tomato Pie

Serves 6 to 8

3 cups sliced peeled tomatoes	2 cups (8 ounces) shredded mild
Salt and pepper to taste	Cheddar cheese
1 cup fresh fine bread crumbs	2 eggs, lightly beaten
1/3 cup thinly sliced onion	3 slices bacon, crisp-cooked and crumbled

Drain the sliced tomatoes on paper towels. Sprinkle with salt and pepper. Sprinkle 1/2 cup of the bread crumbs evenly in a greased 9-inch pie plate. Layer the tomatoes, onion and cheese one-half at a time over the bread crumbs. Pour the eggs over the layers. Sprinkle with salt and pepper. Top with the remaining bread crumbs and the bacon. Bake at 325 degrees on the middle oven rack for 45 minutes.

Melinda Moon Ward

Roasted Root Vegetables with Rosemary

Serves 8

1 pound red potatoes	White and pale green portions of 2 leeks,
1 pound celery root, peeled	cut into 1-inch slices
1 pound carrots, peeled	2 tablespoons fresh rosemary
1 pound rutabagas, peeled	1/2 cup olive oil
1 pound parsnips, peeled	Salt and pepper to taste
2 onions, cut into 1-inch pieces	10 garlic cloves

Position one oven rack in the bottom third and one rack in the center of the oven. Cut the potatoes, celery root, carrots, rutabagas and parsnips into 1-inch cubes. Combine the potatoes, celery root, carrots, rutabagas, parsnips, onions, leeks, rosemary and olive oil in a large bowl and toss to coat. Sprinkle generously with salt and pepper. Divide between two baking sheets sprayed with nonstick cooking spray. Roast at 400 degrees for 30 minutes, stirring occasionally. Reverse the two baking sheets in the oven. Place 5 garlic cloves on each baking sheet and toss to mix. Continue to roast for 45 minutes or until all the vegetables are tender and brown in spots, stirring and turning occasionally. Place in a large serving bowl and serve.

Margaret Bradley McCormick

Roasted Summer Vegetables

Serves 8

6 ears of fresh sweet corn	1 pound fresh whole green beans, trimmed
30 small potatoes, scrubbed	1 tablespoon sea salt
3 tablespoons olive oil	1 teaspoon pepper
30 grape tomatoes	1/2 (4-ounce) package crumbled
25 kalamata olives, drained	goat cheese

Remove the husks and silks from the corn. Cut the kernels from the cobs into a bowl. Cut the potatoes into halves. Drizzle 2 tablespoons of the olive oil in an ovenproof skillet. Place the corn, potatoes, tomatoes, olives and beans in the skillet. Drizzle the remaining 1 tablespoon olive oil over the vegetables. Sprinkle with the sea salt and pepper and toss lightly. Roast at 375 degrees for 30 minutes. Remove from the oven. Add the cheese and toss to mix.

Becky Nye Bickerstaff

Couscous with Mint, Dill and Feta Cheese

Serves 6 to 8

2 cups water	1¹/2 cups chopped unpeeled cucumber
2 tablespoons olive oil	1/3 cup thinly sliced green onions
1 teaspoon kosher salt	1/3 cup lemon juice
1 garlic clove, minced	2 tablespoons chopped fresh mint
1 (10-ounce) package whole wheat couscous	1 tablespoon chopped fresh dill weed, or 1 teaspoon dried dill weed
1 pint cherry tomatoes or grape tomatoes, cut into halves	1 (6-ounce) package crumbled feta cheese
	Salt and pepper to taste

Bring the water, olive oil, kosher salt and garlic to a boil in a medium saucepan. Stir in the couscous gradually. Remove from the heat. Cover and let stand for 5 minutes. Uncover and let stand until cool. Toss the couscous with the remaining ingredients in a bowl. Serve chilled or at room temperature.

Anne Hayes Drinkard Pearce

Ratatouille

Serves 8

1 eggplant, peeled and cut into cubes	1 cup finely chopped fresh parsley
2 zucchini, thinly sliced	1 bay leaf, crumbled
1 onion, chopped	1/2 teaspoon each thyme and marjoram
2 green bell peppers, chopped	1/4 teaspoon each savory and pepper
1/4 cup vegetable oil	1 teaspoon garlic salt
1 (16-ounce) can Italian tomatoes	2 cups (8 ounces) shredded Monterey Jack cheese
4 garlic cloves, minced	
1/4 cup chopped black olives	1 cup (4 ounces) grated Parmesan cheese

Sauté the eggplant, zucchini, onion and bell peppers in the oil in a large skillet until soft. Add the tomatoes, garlic, olives, parsley, bay leaf, thyme, marjoram, savory, pepper and garlic salt and mix well. Simmer, covered, for 30 minutes. Drain off the excess liquid. Sprinkle 1 cup of the Monterey Jack cheese in a greased baking dish. Cover with the vegetable mixture. Sprinkle with the remaining 1 cup Monterey Jack cheese and the Parmesan cheese. Bake at 400 degrees for 20 minutes or until bubbly.

Mary Sprouse Boyd

Ultimate Macaroni and Cheese

Serves 8

1³/4 cups uncooked small elbow macaroni
5 ounces extra-sharp Cheddar cheese, cut into cubes
1²/3 cups all-purpose flour
1¹/2 teaspoons salt
1¹/2 teaspoons dry mustard
1/4 teaspoon black pepper
1/8 teaspoon cayenne pepper

1/8 teaspoon nutmeg
1¹/3 cups half-and-half
1¹/3 cups whipping cream
2/3 cup sour cream
2 eggs, beaten
3/4 teaspoon Worcestershire sauce
5 ounces extra-sharp Cheddar cheese, shredded

Cook the macaroni in water in a saucepan until tender but still firm. Drain and place in a large bowl. Add the cubed cheese and mix well. Whisk the flour, salt, dry mustard, black pepper, cayenne pepper and nutmeg in a large bowl. Whisk in the half-and-half gradually. Whisk in the whipping cream and sour cream gradually. Whisk in the eggs and Worcestershire sauce. Pour over the macaroni mixture and mix well. Spoon into a lightly buttered 9×13-inch glass baking dish. Sprinkle with the shredded cheese. Bake at 350 degrees for 25 minutes or until set around the edges but still jiggles in the center. Remove from the oven. Let stand for 10 minutes to thicken slightly. The sauce will still be creamy when served.

Margaret Bradley McCormick

Baked Almond Rice

Serves 6

1/2 cup (1 stick) butter
1/2 cup uncooked broken vermicelli
1 cup uncooked rice

1/2 cup slivered almonds
2 (10-ounce) cans French onion soup

Melt the butter in a small ovenproof skillet. Add the pasta, rice and almonds. Cook until light brown, stirring constantly. Add the soup. Bake, covered, at 350 degrees for 40 minutes.

Dradyn Coolik Hinson

Artichoke Risotto

Serves 10 to 12

*Jamie Keating is the Executive Chef at the River Mill Café
in Columbus, Georgia, and is a member of the American Culinary Federation
National Culinary Team USA.*

2 shallots, chopped
1 garlic clove, chopped
2 teaspoons olive oil
1 pound uncooked arborio rice
1 quart chicken stock
1 cup heavy cream
2 ounces prosciutto, chopped

1/4 cup (1 ounce) grated pecorino
Romano cheese
Chiffonade of 3 basil leaves
1/4 cup (1/2 stick) unsalted butter
1 (14-ounce) can artichoke hearts,
drained and chopped
Kosher salt and pepper to taste

Sauté the shallots and garlic in the olive oil in a saucepan. Add the rice and toast briefly over low to medium heat, stirring constantly. Add one-third of the stock. Cook until the stock is absorbed, stirring constantly. Repeat twice until all of the stock is absorbed. Add the remaining ingredients and mix well.

Jamie Keating

Baked Asparagus with Rice

Serves 8

1 bunch fresh asparagus, trimmed
2 cups cooked rice
1 (7-ounce) jar pimentos, drained
1 pound sharp Cheddar cheese, shredded

1 1/4 cups slivered almonds
2 (10-ounce) cans cream of chicken soup
1 cup milk
1/2 cup mayonnaise

Cook the asparagus in a steamer. Layer the rice, asparagus, pimentos, one-half of the cheese and the almonds in a large baking dish. Heat the soup, milk and mayonnaise in a saucepan, stirring frequently. Beat until smooth and creamy. Pour over the layers. Sprinkle with the remaining cheese. Bake at 350 degrees for 30 minutes or until bubbly.

Note: Two drained 15-ounce or 19-ounce cans of asparagus can
be substituted for the fresh asparagus.

Jeanie Hinson Bross

Wild and Brown Rice Baked with Apricots

Serves 4

Mitchell Jarrett has not traveled far from his hometown of Columbus to open Mama's Boy in Athens, Georgia, voted best breakfast by the Athens Banner Herald.

2 cups uncooked wild and brown rice blend
3/4 cup fresh orange juice
2 cups broth

1 1/2 cups water
1/2 cup chopped dried apricots
1 teaspoon brown sugar
Pinch of salt and pepper

Mix the rice blend, orange juice, broth, water, apricots, brown sugar, salt and pepper in a bowl. Spoon into a buttered small baking dish. Bake, tightly covered, at 400 degrees for 45 minutes.

Note: For variation, add 1/4 cup pistachio nuts or slivered almonds to the cooked rice mixture.

Mitchell Jarrett, Athens, Georgia

Wild Rice with Mushrooms

Serves 6 to 8

1 cup uncooked wild rice, rinsed and soaked
1/2 cup chopped celery
1/2 cup chopped onion
1/2 cup sliced mushrooms

1/2 cup (1 stick) butter
1/2 teaspoon salt
3 1/2 cups chicken broth or beef broth, heated

Sauté the wild rice, celery, onion and mushrooms in the butter in a skillet for 5 minutes. Stir in the salt. Spoon into a greased baking dish. Pour the hot broth over the top. Bake, covered, at 350 degrees for 1 1/2 hours or until the broth is absorbed.

Note: This recipe can be doubled and baked in two baking dishes.

Catherine Zimmerman Bickerstaff

From Windsors to Wingbacks

Main Dishes & Entrées

Columbus is fortunate to be home to The Springer Opera House, opened in 1871,

once called the finest theater between Washington and New Orleans. Its stage has landed names

such as Ma Rainey, Edwin Booth, Ruth Gordon, and Lillie Langtry, just to name a few.

In 1969, the Junior League of Columbus gave monies to help establish museum rooms

in this National Historic Landmark.

—Janice Persons Biggers

From Windsors to Wingbacks

Main Dishes & Entrées

Blue Cheese and Herb-Stuffed Tenderloin

Serves 8 to 10

1 (7- to 8-pound) beef tenderloin	3 tablespoons chopped parsley
1 (12-ounce) bottle Allegro original marinade	1/4 teaspoon minced garlic
	3 teaspoons dried oregano
4 ounces blue cheese, crumbled	Salt and pepper to taste

Place the beef in a sealable plastic bag. Add the marinade and seal the bag. Marinate in the refrigerator for 4 to 6 hours or longer if desired. Combine the cheese, parsley, garlic and 2 teaspoons of the oregano in a bowl and mix well. Cut a long pocket in the top of the tenderloin to within 1 inch of the bottom, beginning and ending 1/2 inch from the ends. Spoon the cheese mixture into the pocket. Press the sides of the beef together and secure with kitchen string. Rub the remaining 1 teaspoon oregano, salt and pepper on the beef. Place on a rack in a roasting pan. Roast at 425 degrees to 145 degrees on a meat thermometer for medium-rare, 160 degrees for medium or 170 degrees for well done. Roasting time will be about 35 to 45 minutes. Let stand for 5 minutes. Cut the beef into slices and serve.

Christopher Brian Grier

Beef Tenderloin

Serves 10

The smell of this tenderloin cooking will surely bring your guests to the kitchen for a sample. Simply elegant every time and such a Southern classic.

1 beef tenderloin
Salt and pepper to taste
1/4 cup (1/2 stick) butter

Bring the beef to room temperature. Trim the beef of any excess fat. Place on a rack in a baking pan. Sprinkle with salt and pepper. Bake at 450 degrees for 20 minutes. Reduce the oven temperature to 350 degrees. Bake for 15 minutes longer. Remove from the oven and spread the butter over the top. Cover with foil and let stand for 10 to 15 minutes before slicing.

Ruth Combs Flowers

Red Wine-Braised Short Ribs

Serves 4

Chef Cary Taylor draws upon his Southern roots as a Columbus, Georgia, native to bring culinary excellence to the highly acclaimed Chaise Lounge in Chicago, Illinois.

4 pounds boneless short ribs	2 quarts beef stock
1 tablespoon kosher salt, or to taste	1 pound fingerling potatoes
1 carrot, coarsely chopped	1/4 cup olive oil
1 cup coarsely chopped onion	Kosher salt to taste
2 ribs celery, coarsely chopped	2 shallots, thinly sliced
3 sprigs of fresh thyme	1 carrot, thinly sliced
2 bay leaves	2 parsnips, thinly sliced
2 tablespoons black peppercorns	2 ribs celery, thinly sliced
2 cups red wine	2 tablespoons olive oil

Remove the silver skin and fat from the short ribs. Season the short ribs with 1 tablespoon kosher salt. Sear in a skillet over medium-high heat until light brown on all sides. Remove from the skillet. Sauté the chopped carrot, onion, chopped celery, thyme, bay leaves and peppercorns in a skillet until fragrant and caramelized. Place in a large roasting pan and top with the short ribs. Cover with the wine and stock. Bring to a simmer. Cover tightly with foil. Bake at 300 degrees for 4 to 5 hours or until the short ribs are soft and tender. Rub the potatoes with 1/4 cup olive oil and place in a baking dish. Sprinkle with kosher salt to taste. Bake for 1 1/2 hours or until soft. Remove the short ribs from the jus. Strain the jus into a saucepan, discarding the fat and vegetable mixture. Cook until the jus is reduced to a thick sauce.

Sauté the shallots, sliced carrot, parsnips and sliced celery in 2 tablespoons olive oil in a skillet for 5 minutes. Cut the short ribs into four portions. Serve over the potatoes. Garnish with the sautéed vegetables on top. Ladle the sauce over the short ribs and all over the plate.

Cary Taylor, Chicago, Illinois

Savory Chuck Roast

Serves 6 to 8

1 (3-pound) boneless chuck roast
2 tablespoons white vinegar
1 teaspoon garlic salt
1/4 cup all-purpose flour
2 tablespoons olive oil

1/2 envelope onion and mushroom
    soup mix
3/4 cup sherry
1/4 cup brewed coffee
1 cup sliced fresh mushrooms

Rub the beef with the vinegar. Cut eight to ten slits in the beef. Sprinkle the garlic salt into the slits. Dredge the beef in the flour. Brown on all sides in the hot olive oil in a Dutch oven over medium-high heat. Pour a mixture of the soup mix, sherry and coffee over the beef. Add the mushrooms. Bake, covered, at 350 degrees for 1 1/4 hours. Reduce the oven temperature to 300 degrees. Bake for 2 hours longer.

Note: The baking time may vary depending upon the size of the roast. A smaller roast will need to bake at 350 degrees for about 45 minutes and then at 300 degrees for about 2 hours.

Sally Bickerstaff Hatcher

Comfort Beef Stew

Serves 6

1 1/2 pounds stew beef
1 (10-ounce) can golden mushroom soup
1/2 cup sherry
2 carrots, sliced or chopped
1 onion, chopped

4 or 5 small new potatoes
1/2 cup chopped or sliced mushrooms
1/2 green bell pepper, sliced
Hot cooked rice or egg noodles

Place the beef, soup, sherry, carrots and onion in a medium roasting pan. Bake, covered, at 350 degrees for 1 1/2 hours. Remove from the oven. Add the potatoes, mushrooms and bell pepper. Reduce the oven temperature to 300 degrees. Bake for 1 1/2 hours. Serve over the rice.

Martha Gilliam Hatcher

Sweet T's Black Bean Enchiladas

Serves 4

1 onion, chopped
Salt to taste
2 tablespoons olive oil
1 to 1 1/2 pounds ground beef
Dash of ground cumin
2 teaspoons chili powder
Cayenne pepper to taste
Dash of garlic powder
1 envelope fajita seasoning mix
1 (6-ounce) can tomato paste

1 (14-ounce) can stewed tomatoes, or
   1 (10-ounce) can tomatoes and
   green chiles
1 (15-ounce) can black beans,
   drained and rinsed
8 flour tortillas
2 cups (8 ounces) shredded Mexican
   cheese blend
1 to 2 cups sour cream
1 green onion, chopped

Sauté the onion with salt in the olive oil in a skillet until translucent. Add the ground beef. Cook until the ground beef is brown, stirring until crumbly. Add the cumin, chili powder, cayenne pepper and garlic powder. Add the fajita seasoning mix and cook using the package directions. Add the tomato paste and cook until brown. Add the tomatoes and beans. Cook for 15 minutes or until cooked through.

Spoon some of the ground beef mixture down the center of each tortilla. Top with some of the cheese, the sour cream and some of the green onion. Roll up to enclose the filling. Place in a single layer in a large glass baking dish. Spoon one-half of the remaining ground beef mixture over the enchiladas. Sprinkle with one-half of the remaining cheese. Spoon the remaining ground beef mixture over the top. Sprinkle with the remaining cheese and green onion. Bake at 350 degrees for 30 minutes.

Note: You may use 1 cup each of shredded Cheddar cheese and shredded Monterey Jack cheese instead of the Mexican cheese blend.

Teresa Carswell Howard

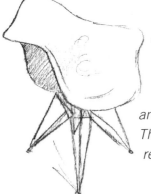

The famous Eames® chair, like the one on the front cover, was first produced by Charles and Ray Eames in the 1940s. The chair has been referred to as the "most famous chair of the century" and has a form that openly welcomes and envelops its occupant, offering a sense of security, warmth, and generosity. These are the feelings that the Junior League of Columbus, Georgia, aspires to render through positive contributions and engagement within our community.

Lasagna

Serves 8 to 10

1 pound hot Italian sausage
8 ounces lean ground beef
2 garlic cloves, minced
1/4 cup chopped fresh basil, or
1 teaspoon dried basil
2 (8-ounce) cans tomato sauce
2 (16-ounce) cans Roma tomatoes
2 (6-ounce) cans tomato paste
1/2 cup minced onion
1 tablespoon sugar

1/4 cup finely chopped fresh parsley, or
2 tablespoons dried parsley
Salt and pepper to taste
1 (10-ounce) package lasagna noodles
1 egg
16 ounces ricotta cheese
1 1/2 teaspoons salt
2 tablespoons parsley, chopped
1 pound mozzarella cheese, sliced
3/4 cup (3 ounces) grated Parmesan cheese

Brown the sausage and ground beef in a skillet, stirring until crumbly; drain. Add the garlic, basil, tomato sauce, tomatoes, tomato paste, onion, sugar and 1/4 cup parsley. Simmer for 30 minutes. Add salt and pepper to taste. Cook the lasagna noodles in boiling salted water in a large saucepan until tender. Drain and rinse. Beat the egg in a bowl. Add the ricotta cheese, 1 1/2 teaspoons salt and 2 tablespoons parsley and mix well.

Spoon 1 1/2 cups of the sauce into a 9×13-inch baking dish. Place one-half of the noodles over the sauce and spread with one-half of the ricotta cheese mixture. Layer one-third of the mozzarella cheese and 1/4 cup of the Parmesan cheese over the layers in the baking dish. Repeat the layers with one-half of the remaining sauce, the remaining noodles, the remaining ricotta cheese mixture and one-half of the remaining mozzarella cheese. Continue layering with the remaining sauce, remaining mozzarella cheese and the remaining 1/2 cup Parmesan cheese. Bake, loosely covered with foil, at 375 degrees for 30 minutes. Remove the foil and bake for 25 minutes longer or until the cheese is light brown on top. Let stand for 10 minutes before serving.

Anne Hayes Drinkard Pearce

Basic Meatballs

Makes 12 meatballs

1 pound ground beef	1/4 cup ketchup
2 eggs	Parsley to taste
1/2 teaspoon pepper	1 cup Italian bread crumbs
1/2 onion, chopped	Vegetable oil for frying
2 ribs celery, chopped	Favorite sauce
2 garlic cloves, minced	

Combine the ground beef, eggs, pepper, onion, celery, garlic, ketchup and parsley in a bowl and mix well. Shape into balls and coat with the bread crumbs. Fry in hot oil in a skillet until golden brown. Drain on paper towels. Simmer in your favorite sauce in a skillet for 1 hour. Serve with spaghetti.

Cathy Powell Hemmings

Meat Loaf

Serves 6

1 to 1 1/2 pounds ground beef	Oregano to taste
1 egg	1 slice white or wheat bread
1 small onion, chopped	1 slice rye or pumpernickel bread
1 tablespoon Worcestershire sauce	1 cup milk
1 teaspoon salt	3 tablespoons grated Parmesan cheese
Pepper to taste	1 (8-ounce) can tomato sauce
Parsley to taste	Oregano for sprinkling

Combine the ground beef, egg, onion, Worcestershire sauce, salt, pepper, parsley and oregano to taste in a bowl and mix well. Tear the bread into pieces. Soak the bread pieces in the milk in a bowl. Strain the bread well by pressing with a fork. Add with the cheese to the ground beef mixture and mix well. Shape into a loaf and place in a 9-ounce loaf pan. Bake at 350 degrees for 30 minutes. Remove from the oven. Spread the tomato sauce over the loaf and sprinkle with oregano. Bake for 15 to 30 minutes or until cooked through.

Gardiner Zollo Church

Spaghetti Pie

Serves 10 to 12

2¹/₂ pounds ground beef
1 cup chopped onion
2 (15-ounce) cans tomato paste
2 (15-ounce) cans tomato sauce
2 tablespoons sugar
¹/₃ cup water
1 tablespoon oregano
Basil and garlic powder to taste

Salt to taste
12 ounces spaghetti, cooked
¹/₂ cup (1 stick) margarine, melted
1 cup (4 ounces) grated Parmesan cheese
3 eggs
2 cups sour cream
8 ounces mozzarella cheese, shredded

Brown the ground beef with the onion in a skillet, stirring until the ground beef is crumbly; drain. Add the tomato paste, tomato sauce, sugar, water, oregano, basil, garlic powder and salt and mix well. Simmer for 30 minutes or longer. Combine the spaghetti, margarine, Parmesan cheese and eggs in a bowl and mix well. Layer the spaghetti mixture, sour cream, ground beef mixture and mozzarella cheese in a 9×13-inch baking dish. Bake at 350 degrees for 35 to 45 minutes or until cooked through. Let stand for 5 to 10 minutes before serving.

Note: This recipe freezes well and can be baked in two smaller baking dishes.

Lu Ann Binns Brandon

Lamb Chops with Mustard Port Sauce

Serves 2

1 rack of lamb, 1 inch thick	3 tablespoons minced onion
1 tablespoon olive oil	1/3 cup tawny port
2 tablespoons chopped rosemary	2/3 cup dry red wine
2 tablespoons coarsely ground pepper	1 cup beef broth
2 tablespoons coarse-grained Dijon mustard	11/2 teaspoons coarse-grained Dijon mustard
1 teaspoon salt	1 tablespoon butter
2 tablespoons olive oil	1 tablespoon all-purpose flour

Cut the rack of lamb into eight 1- to 11/2-inch chops. Combine 1 tablespoon olive oil, the rosemary, pepper, 2 tablespoons Dijon mustard and the salt in a bowl and mix well. Generously coat the lamb chops with the mustard mixture and place in a container. Chill, covered, for 4 to 10 hours.

Heat 2 tablespoons olive oil in a large skillet. Add the lamb chops. Cook for 2 minutes on each side. Cook for 5 to 6 minutes longer for medium-rare. Remove to a plate and cover with foil to keep warm.

Cook the onion in the remaining pan drippings until translucent. Add the port and red wine. Boil until the mixture is reduced by two-thirds. Add the broth. Boil until the mixture is reduced by one-half. Whisk in 11/2 teaspoons Dijon mustard and bring to a boil. Melt the butter in a small saucepan. Stir in the flour until smooth. Stir a small amount of the butter mixture at a time into the sauce, cooking until the desired consistency is achieved. Serve over the lamb chops.

Courtenay Toole Dykes

Panko-Encrusted Rack of Lamb

Serves 4

1/4 cup olive oil
2 tablespoons canola oil
1/2 teaspoon red pepper flakes
8 garlic cloves, minced
1/2 cup thinly sliced scallions
1/2 cup cilantro, minced
1 cup panko (Japanese bread crumbs)

Salt and pepper to taste
1/4 cup mayonnaise
1/2 cup Dijon mustard
1/4 cup soy sauce
2 medium racks of lamb,
   8 ribs each, frenched

Heat the olive oil and canola oil in a skillet over medium heat until hot but not smoking. Stir in the pepper flakes. Stir in the garlic and cook for 30 seconds. Stir in the scallions and cilantro. Add the panko, salt and pepper and mix well. Remove from the heat. Mix the mayonnaise, Dijon mustard and soy sauce in a small bowl.

Heat an ovenproof skillet over high heat. Add the lamb. Sprinkle with salt and pepper. Cook until the sides and ends are evenly brown, turning the lamb occasionally. Drain the skillet. Turn the lamb meat side up. Coat with the mayonnaise mixture and press in the panko mixture evenly. Bake at 450 degrees for 15 to 20 minutes or to 145 degrees on a meat thermometer for medium-rare. Remove to a platter and let stand for 10 minutes before slicing.

James Harris, Grass Creek Lodge, Omaha, Georgia

Pull up a Chair....literally! Upright, that is! Picture this: a very pregnant daughter comes by for a visit, fixes herself a very large serving of ice cream, and plops down in a comfy, rocking club chair. Leaning back for the fullest possible pleasure of snuggle and slurp, she's suddenly dumped in a backward somersault! With chair and daughter in upright positions (and assurance that the baby was not arriving on the spot), it became a giggly good time.

—Margaret Glenn Zollo

Herb-Baked Pork Roast

Serves 6 to 8

1/2 cup soy sauce
1/2 cup vegetable oil
2 tablespoons lemon juice
2 garlic cloves, minced
2 tablespoons Italian seasoning
1 teaspoon pepper
1 (3- to 4-pound) boneless pork loin roast

Mix the soy sauce, oil, lemon juice, garlic, Italian seasoning and pepper in a sealable plastic bag. Add the pork and seal the bag. Marinate in the refrigerator for 8 to 10 hours. Place the pork and the marinade in a baking dish. Bake, tightly covered with foil, for 2 hours or to 160 degrees on a meat thermometer.

Katherine Ramsey Maxey

Tomato Pork Chops

Serves 4

*Brown the pork chops with salt and pepper to help seal in the flavor.
An excellent, easy meal to serve on a cold winter's day.*

4 pork chops
1 teaspoon salt
Pepper to taste
2 (10-ounce) cans tomato soup
1 onion, sliced
1 green bell pepper, sliced
1 red bell pepper, sliced

Sprinkle the pork chops with the salt and pepper. Brown the pork chops lightly in a skillet over medium heat. Add the soup and onion. Cover and reduce the heat. Simmer for 2 hours or longer or until the pork chops are tender, stirring occasionally. Add the bell peppers during the last 30 minutes of the cooking time.

Olivia Cheves Blanchard

Marinated Pork Tenderloin

Serves 16

1/2 cup soy sauce	1/2 teaspoon pepper
1/2 cup teriyaki sauce	1 tablespoon olive oil
3 tablespoons brown sugar	2 green onions, chopped
1 garlic clove, minced	4 pork tenderloins

Combine the soy sauce, teriyaki sauce, brown sugar, garlic, pepper, olive oil and green onions in a bowl and mix well. Pour over the pork in a sealable plastic bag and seal the bag. Marinate in the refrigerator for 4 to 10 hours. Drain the pork, discarding the marinade. Place the pork in a baking pan. Bake at 325 degrees for 1 hour or until cooked through.

Note: The marinated pork can be placed on a grill rack and grilled over medium-high heat for 20 minutes or until cooked through.

Barbara Hamby Swift

Pork with Mushrooms

Serves 4

1 teaspoon rice wine or dry sherry	1 bunch green onions, sliced
1/2 teaspoon minced fresh ginger	2 tablespoons vegetable oil
2 tablespoons soy sauce	2 garlic cloves, minced
1/4 teaspoon sugar	8 ounces fresh mushrooms, thickly sliced
1/2 teaspoon cornstarch	1 teaspoon cornstarch
1/4 teaspoon pepper	5 tablespoons water
8 ounces ground pork	4 cups white rice, cooked

Combine the wine, ginger, soy sauce, sugar, 1/2 teaspoon cornstarch and the pepper in a small bowl and mix well. Add the pork and coat with the marinade. Marinate for 10 minutes. Arrange the green onions on a platter. Heat the oil in a wok. Add the garlic and stir-fry until brown. Discard the garlic. Add the pork and stir-fry for 4 minutes or until brown. Remove the pork with a slotted spoon and place on top of the green onions to steam. Reduce the heat to medium. Add the mushrooms and stir-fry for 4 minutes or until soft. Dissolve 1 teaspoon cornstarch in the water in a cup to form a paste. Add the paste, pork and green onions to the wok. Stir-fry for 1 minute. Serve hot over the rice.

Jennifer Gillespie Daniel

Sausage and Pasta Bake

Serves 6

8 ounces ziti or mostaccioli
1 pound mild or hot Italian sausage
1 large onion, coarsely chopped
2 garlic cloves, minced
1 large red bell pepper, cut into 1-inch squares
1 large green bell pepper, cut into 1-inch squares
1 (14-ounce) can diced tomatoes
1 (6-ounce) can tomato paste
1/4 cup fresh basil
2 cups (8 ounces) shredded Italian 6-cheese blend

Cook the pasta using the package directions; drain. Cut the sausage into 1-inch pieces and discard the casings. Cook in a 12-inch skillet over medium heat until brown on all sides; drain. Add the onion, garlic and bell peppers. Cook for 5 minutes or until the sausage is cooked through and the vegetables are tender-crisp. Add the undrained tomatoes and tomato paste and mix well. Stir in the pasta and basil. Spoon into a 9×13-inch baking dish. Bake, covered with foil, at 375 degrees for 20 minutes. Uncover and sprinkle evenly with the cheese to cover the top. Bake for 5 minutes or until the cheese melts.

Jane Durden Etheridge

Enjoying an afternoon sitting outside waving to neighbors is as Southern as fried chicken and sweet tea. Our weather is ideal for this pastime and is exactly where you would find Charles "Beanie" Morgan most afternoons. Sitting in his customary wrought iron chair, Beanie would throw up his hand in the most cordial fashion as each of us would drive by. He was a staple to the neighbors of Hilton Heights and as word spread of his passing, friends and neighbors surrounded his "chair" with bouquets of flowers in honor of Southern hospitality.

— Millie Peacock Patrick

Praline Chicken

Serves 6

Serve with angel hair pasta and grated Parmesan cheese.

Chicken
8 ounces cream cheese, softened
1 cup (4 ounces) grated Parmesan cheese
2 tablespoons chopped green onions
1/4 teaspoon nutmeg
6 boneless skinless chicken breasts, cut into halves lengthwise
1 cup bread crumbs
1 cup (4 ounces) grated Parmesan cheese

Praline Sauce
1 (12-ounce) jar honey
2 tablespoons butter
1/3 cup spicy mustard
1/3 cup Dijon mustard
1/2 to 1 cup pecans

To prepare the chicken, mix the cream cheese, 1 cup Parmesan cheese, the green onions and nutmeg in a bowl. Place a small amount on each chicken slice and roll up, folding the sides in. Mix the bread crumbs and 1 cup Parmesan cheese in a bowl. Coat the roll-ups with the bread crumb mixture. Place tightly together in an 8×8-inch baking dish sprayed with nonstick cooking spray. Bake at 350 degrees for 30 to 40 minutes or until brown on top. (Some of the cheese may spill out and will be bubbly.)

To prepare the sauce, heat the honey, butter, spicy mustard and Dijon mustard in a saucepan over medium-low heat until the butter melts and the mixture is smooth, stirring constantly. Do not boil. Stir in the pecans. Spoon over the chicken roll-ups at serving time.

Fran Martin Sessions

Gourmet Chicken and Herb Pizza

Serves 16 (makes 2 pizzas)

1 envelope fast-rising yeast or regular yeast
1 1/4 cups warm water
1 tablespoon sugar
2 tablespoons vegetable oil
3 to 3 1/2 cups all-purpose flour
2 teaspoons minced garlic
2 1/2 cups chopped onions
2 teaspoons oregano
2 teaspoons basil
2 tablespoons finely chopped fresh cilantro

1/2 cup (1 stick) butter
2 tablespoons olive oil
4 boneless skinless chicken breasts
Salt and pepper to taste
2 cups sliced fresh mushrooms
2 cups (8 ounces) grated Parmesan cheese
1 cup crumbled basil and tomato feta cheese
2 cups (8 ounces) shredded mozzarella cheese

Sprinkle the yeast over the water in a bowl. Let stand for a few minutes or until the yeast begins to dissolve. Add the sugar and vegetable oil. Add 3 cups of the flour 1 cup at a time, stirring well after each addition. Add the remaining 1/2 cup flour if needed to form a firm dough. Place in an oiled bowl, turning to coat the surface. Let rise for 20 to 30 minutes or until doubled in bulk.

Sauté 1 teaspoon of the garlic, 1 cup of the onions, the oregano, basil and 1 tablespoon of the cilantro in the butter in a skillet until the onion is translucent. Chill until congealed.

Divide the dough into two equal portions. Roll each portion to the desired thickness on a lightly floured surface with a floured rolling pin. Brush with the olive oil. Spread each portion with half the congealed butter mixture.

Pan-fry the chicken in the remaining 1 teaspoon garlic, 1 cup of the remaining onions, salt and pepper in a skillet until the chicken is cooked through. Shred the chicken. Sprinkle equal portions of the chicken, mushrooms, remaining 1/2 cup onion, the Parmesan cheese, feta cheese and mozzarella cheese on each pizza. Grill on a pizza stone in a ceramic smoker at 300 degrees for 10 to 15 minutes or until the crust is brown. Garnish with the remaining 1 tablespoon cilantro. The pizzas can be baked at 375 degrees for 10 to 15 minutes or grilled on a charcoal grill.

Note: Packaged pizza dough may be used and can be found in the bakery section or refrigerator section of your grocery store. Decrease the topping ingredients by one-half if only one pizza is prepared.

Christopher Brian Grier

Country Captain

Serves 4

1 (2- to 3-pound) chicken or chicken pieces
All-purpose flour for coating
Salt and black pepper to taste
Vegetable oil for frying
2 onions, finely chopped
2 green bell peppers, chopped
1 or 2 garlic cloves, crushed
1 teaspoon (heaping) salt
1/2 teaspoon white pepper

2 teaspoons curry powder
2 (16-ounce) cans tomatoes
1 teaspoon chopped parsley
1/2 teaspoon ground thyme
Sugar (optional)
Chicken stock (optional)
2 cups cooked rice
3 tablespoons currants
4 ounces slivered almonds, toasted
Parsley for garnish

Coat the chicken with a mixture of flour, salt and black pepper. Fry in hot oil in a skillet until brown and cooked through. Remove from the skillet and keep hot. (This is the secret of the dish's success.)

Drain the skillet, reserving a small amount of the drippings. Add the onions, bell peppers and garlic. Cook over low heat, stirring constantly. Add 1 teaspoon salt, the white pepper and curry powder. Adjust the seasonings to taste. Stir in the tomatoes, 1 teaspoon parsley, the thyme and black pepper. (Many canned tomatoes are too acidic, so be sure to taste the sauce after mixing. If desired, add a very small quantity of sugar to cut the acid.)

Place the chicken in a roasting pan and pour the sauce over the top. (If there is not enough sauce to cover the chicken, rinse out the skillet and heat some chicken stock to pour over the chicken also.) Bake, covered, at 350 degrees for 45 minutes.

Place the chicken in the center of a serving platter and surround with the rice. Mix the currants into the sauce and pour over the rice. Scatter the almonds over the top. Garnish with parsley. Spoon any extra sauce into a gravy boat.

Note: The dish known as Country Captain was created by Mary Blackmar Bullard in the early 1900s. Miss Mamie, as she was affectionately called, shared her recipe and her love for entertaining with her daughters, Mira and Louise, who in turn shared the dish with Columbus friends and special guests. Legend has it that General George Patton so enjoyed Country Captain that he requested delivery of a supply of this delicacy at his departure on a troop train during World War II, pulling up his train car chair to receive the yummy bucketful right through the window! President Franklin Delano Roosevelt was another guest of this family who enjoyed the Country Captain so much that he hired Julius, the family cook, to move with him to the White House.

Mira Bullard Hart

Firehouse Chicken and Dumplings

A favorite of our firefighter friends.

Serves 6

3 quarts water
1 (3- to 4-pound) chicken
1 onion, cut into quarters
1 rib celery, chopped
2 garlic cloves, cut into halves
2 bay leaves
2 cups all-purpose flour
1 1/2 teaspoons baking powder
1/2 teaspoon salt, or to taste

Bring the water to a boil in a heavy saucepan. Add the chicken, onion, celery, garlic and bay leaves. Cook, uncovered, for 1 1/2 hours. Remove from the heat. Remove the chicken from the saucepan to cool. Strain the stock, discarding the solids. Chop the chicken, discarding the skin and bones.

Mix the flour, baking powder and salt in a bowl. Stir in 1 cup of the stock until smooth. Let stand for 10 minutes. Roll the dough 1/4 inch thick on a floured surface. Cut into 1-inch squares.

Heat 6 cups of the remaining stock in a large heavy saucepan over medium heat. Add the chicken. Drop the dumpling squares one at a time into the hot stock to keep them from sticking together. Simmer for 30 minutes or until the stock thickens, stirring constantly to keep the dumplings from sticking to the bottom of the saucepan.

Edie Pendleton Evans

"*Money cannot buy health, but I'd settle for a diamond-studded wheelchair.*"

—*Dorothy Parker*

Chicken and Spinach Lasagna

Serves 12

4 ounces mushrooms	1/4 teaspoon nutmeg
2 tablespoons butter	1/2 teaspoon salt
2 cups chopped cooked chicken	1/4 teaspoon pepper
10 ounces fresh spinach, chopped, or	1 tablespoon soy sauce
1 (10-ounce) package frozen spinach,	1 cup cream of mushroom soup
thawed and drained well	1 cup sour cream
2 cups (8 ounces) shredded	1/3 cup mayonnaise
Cheddar cheese	6 no-boil lasagna noodles
1/2 cup finely chopped onion	1 cup (4 ounces) grated Parmesan cheese

Sauté the mushrooms in the butter in a skillet until tender. Combine the chicken, spinach, sautéed mushrooms, Cheddar cheese, onion, nutmeg, salt, pepper, soy sauce, soup, sour cream and mayonnaise in a large bowl and mix well. Layer the noodles, chicken mixture and Parmesan cheese one-half at a time in a 9×13-inch baking dish. Bake at 350 degrees for 50 minutes.

Allison Weaver Peak

Creamy Chicken Enchiladas

Serves 6

1 tablespoon butter	4 cups chopped cooked chicken
1 onion, chopped	8 (8-inch) flour tortillas
1 (4-ounce) can chopped green chiles, drained	1 pound Monterey Jack cheese, shredded
8 ounces cream cheese, chopped and softened	2 cups whipping cream

Melt the butter in a skillet over medium heat. Add the onion and sauté for 5 minutes. Add the green chiles and sauté for 1 minute. Stir in the cream cheese and chicken. Cook until the cream cheese melts, stirring constantly. Spoon 2 to 3 tablespoons of the chicken mixture down the center of each tortilla. Roll up and place seam side down in a lightly greased 9×13-inch baking dish. Sprinkle with the Monterey Jack cheese and drizzle with the cream. Bake at 350 degrees for 45 minutes. Cut into squares to serve.

Jennifer Daniel Harper

Orange Marmalade Cornish Hens

Serves 4

1/2 cup orange marmalade	2 tablespoons butter, melted
1/2 cup quince jelly	2 tablespoons olive oil
1 teaspoon soy sauce	Salt and freshly cracked
4 Cornish game hens	pepper to taste

Combine the marmalade, jelly and soy sauce in a heavy saucepan. Bring to a boil and reduce the heat to a simmer.

Brush the hens with the butter and olive oil. Sprinkle with salt and pepper. Place in a baking pan. Broil for 5 to 10 minutes or until light brown. Reduce the oven temperature to 350 degrees. Bake the hens to 165 degrees on a meat thermometer, brushing with the some of the marmalade sauce during the last 15 minutes. Return the remaining marmalade sauce to a boil. Boil for 2 minutes. Serve on the side.

Laura Schomburg Patrick

Dijon-Rubbed Turkey

Serves 10 to 12

This is a great recipe for cooks who have always been afraid to roast their own turkey for Thanksgiving. Once you try it, you'll never buy another cooked turkey.

1 cup Dijon mustard
3/4 cup olive oil
1/2 cup fresh parsley, chopped
1/3 cup fresh lemon juice
2 tablespoons lemon zest
1 tablespoon chopped fresh thyme
1 tablespoon chopped fresh sage
1 (15- to 16-pound) fresh turkey

21/2 cups canned chicken broth or low-sodium chicken broth
8 ounces chopped fresh mushrooms
11/4 cups chicken broth
1/2 cup whipping cream
2 tablespoons cornstarch
Salt and pepper to taste

Mix the Dijon mustard, olive oil, parsley, lemon juice, lemon zest, thyme and sage in a bowl. Reserve 1/2 cup of the mustard mixture in a bowl in the refrigerator. Rub the remaining mustard mixture over the turkey breast and under the skin, carefully replacing the skin. Chill, covered, for 24 to 48 hours. Rub the reserved mustard mixture over the surface of the turkey.

Place the turkey in a large roasting pan. Roast at 325 degrees for 1 hour. Baste the turkey with 1/2 cup of the 21/2 cups broth and tent loosely with foil. Roast for 3 hours or until a meat thermometer inserted into the thickest portion of the thigh registers 175 degrees, basting frequently with the remaining 2 cups broth. Remove the turkey to a platter and tent with foil, reserving the pan drippings.

Pour the reserved pan drippings into a 4-cup liquid measure. Remove the fat with a spoon, reserving 2 tablespoons of the fat. Place the reserved fat in a skillet. Add the mushrooms and sauté until tender. Add enough of the 11/4 cups chicken broth to the reserved pan drippings to measure 3 cups. Pour into the mushroom mixture and stir in the cream. Boil for 8 minutes. Dissolve the cornstarch in 2 tablespoons of the remaining broth and add to the gravy. Cook until thickened, stirring constantly to prevent lumps. Season with salt and pepper. Carve the turkey and serve with the gravy.

Anne Hayes Drinkard Pearce

Crab Cakes

Makes 9 crab cakes

Shape into miniature crab cakes and serve as an appetizer.

1 pound crab meat, shells removed
and crab meat flaked
3 green onions with tops, finely chopped
1/2 cup finely chopped bell pepper
1/4 cup mayonnaise
1/2 cup butter crackers, crushed
1 egg
1 teaspoon salt

1 teaspoon dry mustard
1/4 teaspoon garlic powder
Juice of 1/2 lemon
1/8 teaspoon cayenne pepper
1 teaspoon Worcestershire sauce
1/2 cup all-purpose flour
1/2 cup peanut oil

Combine the crab meat, green onions, bell pepper, mayonnaise, cracker crumbs, egg, salt, dry mustard, garlic powder, lemon juice, cayenne pepper and Worcestershire sauce in a bowl and mix well. Shape into nine patties and place on a platter. Chill for 2 hours. Dust the crab cakes lightly with the flour. Fry in the hot peanut oil in a skillet over medium to medium-low heat for 4 to 5 minutes or until golden brown on the bottom. Turn and fry until golden brown.

Sara Stola Evans

"Can-Can's" Crab Imperial

Serves 4

1 pound crab meat, shells removed
and crab meat flaked
1 teaspoon dry mustard
1/2 teaspoon salt

1 teaspoon Worcestershire sauce
1/2 cup mayonnaise
1 tablespoon capers
Hot cooked rice

Combine the crab meat, dry mustard, salt, Worcestershire sauce, mayonnaise and capers in a bowl and mix well. Spoon into a buttered baking dish. Bake at 375 degrees for 20 minutes. Serve over rice.

Jennings Adams DeWitt Palmer

Crab Ravioli in Creamy Tomato Sauce

Serves 8

6 ounces lump crab meat
4 ounces ricotta cheese
1 teaspoon Italian seasoning
1 (12-ounce) package won ton wrappers
1 egg, beaten
All-purpose flour for dusting
1 cup milk
1 envelope creamy tomato sauce mix
2 tablespoons butter
Salt to taste
Chopped parsley for sprinkling

Drain the crab meat, reserving the liquid. Combine the crab meat, ricotta cheese and Italian seasoning in a bowl and mix well. Brush the won ton wrappers with the egg. Place about 1/2 teaspoon crab meat filling in the center of each won ton wrapper. Fold each to form a triangle and press the edges to seal. Place on a flour-dusted baking sheet.

Combine the milk and reserved crab liquid in a large saucepan. Whisk in the tomato sauce mix. Add the butter. Bring to a boil over medium-high heat and reduce the heat. Simmer for 3 minutes, stirring frequently. Keep warm over low heat.

Fill a large saucepan with salted water and bring to a boil. Drop the ravioli in batches of eight into the boiling water. Cook for 2 minutes or until the ravioli rise to the surface. Carefully remove the ravioli to the sauce with a slotted spoon. Sprinkle with the parsley and serve.

Lisa McMullen Allen

Several American towns are involved in a battle over the title of World's Largest Chair. Miller's Office Furniture in Anniston, Alabama, built a thirty-one-foot-tall office chair in a vacant lot next to its store and is believed to be the current title holder.

Baton Rouge Shrimp Étouffée

Serves 8

½ cup (1 stick) butter
⅓ cup all-purpose flour
½ cup (1 stick) butter
1 cup finely chopped green onion bulbs
2 cups finely chopped onions
3 garlic cloves, minced
1 cup finely chopped bell pepper
1 cup finely chopped celery
2 bay leaves
¼ cup thyme, finely chopped
½ teaspoon finely chopped sweet basil
½ teaspoon white pepper

2 teaspoons salt
2 tablespoons Worcestershire sauce
1 teaspoon Louisiana hot sauce
1 cup dry wine
2 cups clamato juice or chicken broth
5 pounds shrimp, peeled and deveined
1 tablespoon lemon juice
1 tablespoon grated lemon zest
¼ cup parsley, chopped
½ cup chopped green onions
Hot cooked rice

Melt ½ cup butter in a heavy Dutch oven over medium heat. Stir in the flour to form a roux, stirring constantly. Add ½ cup butter, the green onion bulbs, onions, garlic, bell pepper, celery, bay leaves, thyme and basil and sauté for 20 minutes. Add the white pepper, salt, Worcestershire sauce, hot sauce, wine and clamato juice and mix well. Bring to a boil and reduce the heat. Simmer, uncovered, for 1 hour, stirring occasionally. Add the shrimp, lemon juice, lemon zest, parsley and green onions. Cook over medium heat for 15 minutes or until the shrimp turn pink. Do not overcook. Discard the bay leaves. Serve over rice.

Note: The shrimp will overcook quickly. Be careful when reheating and do not heat longer than necessary.

Robert M. Culver, Jr., Baton Rouge, Louisiana

Curried Shrimp and Rice

Serves 8

2 to 2$\frac{1}{2}$ pounds fresh shrimp, peeled and deveined
2 tablespoons olive oil
2 tablespoons white wine
2 teaspoons Old Bay seasoning
$\frac{1}{2}$ cup (1 stick) margarine
1 small onion, chopped
1 red bell pepper, chopped

3 ribs celery, chopped
1$\frac{1}{2}$ teaspoons curry powder
1 teaspoon white pepper
$\frac{1}{2}$ teaspoon salt
$\frac{1}{2}$ cup chopped almonds
$\frac{3}{4}$ cup dark or golden raisins
1$\frac{1}{2}$ cups brown rice, cooked
6 slices bacon, crisp-cooked and crumbled

Sauté the shrimp in the olive oil, wine and Old Bay seasoning in a skillet over medium heat for 8 to 10 minutes or until the shrimp are just barely pink. Remove from the heat. Melt the margarine in a large sauté pan. Add the onion, bell pepper, celery, curry powder, white pepper, salt, almonds and raisins and sauté until the vegetables are softened. Remove from the heat. Add the shrimp and rice and mix well. Spoon into a 9×11-inch baking dish. Sprinkle with the bacon. Bake at 350 degrees for 30 minutes.

Amelia Alcorn Vaught

Shrimp and Grits

Serves 6

The quintessential Southern dish...grits! We love our grits served with cheese, bacon, chives, and of course shrimp. For an added flair, serve your grits in a martini glass and garnish with the topping of your choice.

2 cups chopped shallots
1 teaspoon chopped garlic
1 cup (2 sticks) butter
1 cup all-purpose flour
8 cups chicken stock
2 roasted red bell peppers, chopped

2 jalapeño chiles, chopped
$\frac{1}{2}$ teaspoon white pepper, or to taste
3 pounds medium shrimp
Juice of 2 lemons
Hot cooked grits

Sauté the shallots and garlic in the butter in a saucepan until translucent. Stir in the flour. Add the stock, roasted peppers and jalapeño chiles. Simmer until the liquid is reduced. Sprinkle with the white pepper. Add the shrimp. Heat until the shrimp turn pink. Stir in the lemon juice. Serve over grits.

Barbara Hamby Swift

Shrimp Pasta with White Wine Caper Sauce

Serves 4

1/4 cup (1/2 stick) butter
1/4 cup extra-virgin olive oil
2 large shallots, coarsely chopped
2 or 3 large garlic cloves, minced
Salt, white pepper and black pepper to taste
1 cup white wine
1 pound shrimp, peeled and deveined
1 1/2 tablespoons capers
8 ounces angel hair pasta, cooked
Freshly grated Parmesan cheese for topping (optional)
White truffle oil or good-quality olive oil for drizzling (optional)

Melt the butter with the olive oil in a large sauté pan over medium-low heat. Add the shallots and cook until tender. Add the garlic and cook for 2 to 3 minutes. Sprinkle with salt, white pepper and black pepper. Add the wine. Cook until the wine is reduced by one-half. Add the shrimp and capers. Cook for 4 to 5 minutes or until the shrimp turn pink. Add the pasta and toss to coat. Top with cheese and drizzle with truffle oil.

Teresa Carswell Howard

*W*hen we went to my grandparents' house, my brother and I would race to get out of the car to run to my grandfather's brown leather club chair in the living room. My grandfather, "Big Daddy," would act like he was a big, mean man. Booming in a deep voice, he would say, "GET OUT OF MY CHAIR!" We would giggle and laugh while he grabbed our ankles and held us upside down, swinging.

— *Kathleen Wren Gilliam*

Shrimp and Sausage Jambalaya

Serves 8

Even though we don't live on the bayou, our Cajun friends have had a huge influence on our Southern cuisine. Nothing is better to share with your supper club than a bowl of Shrimp and Sausage Jambalaya.

1 pound andouille or smoked sausage, sliced
1 cup chopped onion
3/4 cup chopped green bell pepper
3 garlic cloves, minced
1 (16-ounce) can tomatoes
1 tablespoon Creole seasoning
1/2 teaspoon salt
1/4 teaspoon marjoram
1/4 teaspoon cayenne pepper
1/4 teaspoon black pepper
1 bay leaf
1 cup chicken broth
1 cup converted rice
2 tablespoons chopped fresh parsley
1 pound fresh shrimp, peeled

Sauté the sausage in a heavy 4-quart stockpot until light brown on all sides. Remove the sausage from the stockpot to drain. Sauté the onion, bell pepper and garlic in the drippings in the stockpot until tender. Add the undrained tomatoes, Creole seasoning, salt, marjoram, cayenne pepper, black pepper, bay leaf, broth, sausage and rice. Bring to a boil, stirring occasionally. Reduce the heat to medium-low. Cook until most of the liquid is absorbed, stirring occasionally. Add the parsley and shrimp. Simmer, covered, for 25 minutes, stirring occasionally.

Edie Pendleton Evans

Sherried Cod in Parchment

Serves 2

2 frozen cod fillets	1 Vidalia onion, thinly sliced
1 tablespoon olive oil	1 tablespoon minced garlic
Salt-free spicy seasoning to taste	2 tablespoons sherry
Salt-free lemon pepper to taste	1 tablespoon lemon juice
Sea salt or kosher salt to taste	2 tablespoons soft bread crumbs (optional)
1 tablespoon olive oil	Freshly ground black pepper to taste

Brush the tops and bottoms of the fillets with 1 tablespoon olive oil. Sprinkle the bottom of each fillet with spicy seasoning and the top with lemon pepper. Sprinkle with sea salt and set aside.

Heat 1 tablespoon olive oil in a sauté pan over medium heat. Add the onion and cook until almost translucent. Add the garlic. Place the fillets on top of the onion mixture. Cook until the fillets begin to warm, pushing the onion to the side of the pan. Sear the fillets until light brown on each side. Remove the pan from the heat.

Place the fillets right side up on a sheet of baking parchment about twice the length of the baking dish, keeping the onions in the pan. Return the pan to the heat. Add the sherry and heat until warm. Add the lemon juice. Pour over the fillets. Bring two sides of the baking parchment over the fillets and fold over and down together. Continue folding until all the open edges are folded in. Twist the ends and tuck under. Place in the baking dish. Bake at 400 degrees for 25 minutes. Open the baking parchment carefully so the steam can escape. Sprinkle with the bread crumbs. Broil until brown and sprinkle with black pepper. Cut the baking time in half if using thawed cod fillets.

Shari Phipps Evans

Wasabi Salmon

Serves 2

1/4 cup low-sodium soy sauce	1 teaspoon dark sesame oil
1 teaspoon wasabi powder	2 salmon fillets
1 1/2 teaspoons minced fresh ginger	

Mix the soy sauce, wasabi powder, ginger and sesame oil in a sealable plastic bag. Add the fillets and seal the bag, turning to coat. Marinate in the refrigerator for 2 to 3 hours. Place the fillets and the marinade in a greased 8×8-inch baking dish. Bake at 350 degrees for 35 to 40 minutes or until the fillets flake easily.

Dori Sponcler Jones

Salmon Piccata

Serves 4

4 salmon fillets, boned	4 ounces cured Spanish capers
1 teaspoon salt	Juice of 1/2 lemon
1 teaspoon pepper	1 1/4 cups water
1 tablespoon butter	1 tablespoon olive oil
2 tablespoons olive oil	1 cup uncooked garlic and herb couscous
Juice of 1 lemon	1/2 lemon, cut into 4 thin slices
1/4 cup chopped cilantro	Chopped cilantro for garnish
1/4 cup chardonnay	Lime wedges for garnish
1/4 cup chicken stock	

Sprinkle the fillets with the salt and pepper. Melt the butter with 2 tablespoons olive oil in a large nonstick skillet. Place the fillets skin side up in the skillet. Cook for 3 minutes on each side, basting with the butter mixture after turning. Squeeze the juice of 1 lemon over the fillets and remove from the skillet. Sprinkle the fillets with 1/4 cup cilantro and let stand. Do not cover.

Pour the wine into the pan drippings. Cook until reduced, stirring to deglaze the skillet. Add the stock. Cook over medium heat, stirring constantly. Add the capers and the juice of 1/2 lemon. Cook for 5 minutes to reduce. Return the fillets to the skillet, basting with the sauce for full flavor.

Bring the water and 1 tablespoon olive oil to a boil in a saucepan. Add the seasoning packet from the couscous. Remove from the heat. Stir in the couscous gently. Cover and let stand for 8 minutes. Stir gently with a fork and cover again.

Create a bed of couscous on a platter. Place each fillet diagonally on the couscous. Place one lemon slice on each fillet. Pour the reduction sauce over the fillets, placing as many capers as possible on each fillet. Garnish with cilantro and lime wedges.

Maggie Victoria Johnston

"*Musical chairs*" *is a metaphor for shuffling people or items among various locations.*

Sautéed Prosciutto Gulf Red Snapper with Asparagus and Herb Butter

Serves 2

Jamie Gruber, Executive Chef at The Market, located in downtown Columbus, enjoys sharing his take on fresh fish dishes.

1 (8-ounce) Gulf red snapper fillet
2 or 3 slices prosciutto
Salt and pepper to taste
2 tablespoons (about) olive oil
3 1/2 tablespoons butter
1 bunch asparagus spears, blanched
1 garlic clove, chopped
1/2 cup chopped fresh herbs
Splash of white wine

Pat the fillet dry. Wrap the prosciutto around the fillet with the ends meeting on the flesh side of the fish. Sprinkle with salt and pepper. Heat an ovenproof skillet over medium-high heat. Add enough of the olive oil to cover the bottom of the skillet. Add 1 tablespoon of the butter and heat until melted. Place the fillet flesh side down in the mixture. Cook for 4 to 5 minutes or until golden brown. Turn the fillet and place the skillet in the oven. Bake at 400 degrees for 4 to 5 minutes or until the fillet flakes easily.

Sauté the asparagus and garlic in 2 tablespoons of the remaining butter in a sauté pan for 3 to 5 minutes or until heated through. Melt the remaining 1/2 tablespoon butter with the herbs, wine, salt and pepper in a small saucepan. Turn off the heat. Place the asparagus in the center of a plate and lay the fillet on top. Spoon the herb butter over the fillet.

Jamie Gruber

Artichoke-Encrusted Tilapia

Serves 4

1/2 cup artichokes, drained and chopped
1/4 cup chopped red and green bell pepper
1/4 cup chopped scallions
1/4 cup Italian salad dressing

1 sleeve butter crackers, crushed
1/4 cup (1 ounce) grated Parmesan cheese
4 tilapia fillets

Combine the artichokes, bell pepper, scallions, salad dressing, cracker crumbs and cheese in a bowl and mix well. Place the fillets in a glass baking dish sprayed with nonstick cooking spray. Spoon the artichoke mixture on top of the fillets. Bake at 350 degrees for 18 to 20 minutes or until the fillets flake easily.

Amy Giuliano Adams

Crepes aux Champignons

Serves 6

This recipe is a personal favorite of Chef Marcel Carles. Marcel is a talented chef originally from Paris, France, who has been sharing his culinary talents in Columbus, Georgia, for over forty years.

3/4 cup all-purpose flour
1 1/2 teaspoons vegetable oil
Pinch of salt
1 cup milk
1 egg

3/4 cup (1 1/2 sticks) butter
7 ounces fresh mushrooms
Salt and pepper to taste
1 tablespoon all-purpose flour
2 cups whipping cream

Mix 3/4 cup flour, the oil and a pinch of salt in a bowl. Add 1/2 cup of the milk and mix well. Stir in the remaining 1/2 cup milk and the egg. Heat 1/4 cup of the butter in a skillet until melted. Ladle 1 ounce of the batter into the skillet, tilting to coat evenly. Cook until the edge begins to curl. Turn and cook until the top is light brown. Slide the crepe onto a plate. Repeat the process, adding an additional 1/4 cup of the remaining butter after the first three crepes are made. This recipe makes six crepes.

Cut the mushrooms into slices. Melt the remaining 1/4 cup butter in a heavy skillet. Add the mushrooms and salt and pepper to taste. Sauté for 5 minutes. Sprinkle with 1 tablespoon flour. Add the cream and simmer for 5 minutes, stirring frequently. Fill each crepe with the mushroom mixture and roll to enclose the filling.

Marcel Carles

Eggplant Parmigiana

Serves 6

1 eggplant	1 (15-ounce) can tomato sauce
3 or 4 egg whites, lightly beaten	1 teaspoon Italian seasoning
2 cups seasoned bread crumbs	1/2 teaspoon basil
1 tablespoon olive oil	1/4 teaspoon oregano
1 onion, sliced	1/2 teaspoon salt
3 garlic cloves	1/4 teaspoon pepper
1 cup sliced fresh mushrooms	1 teaspoon sugar
Olive oil for sautéing	15 ounces ricotta cheese
1 (28-ounce) can crushed tomatoes in purée	1/4 cup (1 ounce) grated Parmesan cheese
	6 ounces mozzarella cheese, shredded

Cut the eggplant into halves lengthwise. Cut each half into 1/4-inch slices. Dip into the egg whites and dredge in the bread crumbs to coat. Place in a single layer on two baking sheets sprayed with nonstick cooking spray. Drizzle with 1 tablespoon olive oil. Wrap the onion and garlic in foil. Bake the eggplant with the foil packet at 375 degrees for 40 minutes, turning the eggplant once.

Sauté the mushrooms in olive oil in a skillet for 5 minutes. Combine the tomatoes, tomato sauce, Italian seasoning, basil, oregano, salt, pepper and sugar in a medium saucepan and mix well. Bring to a boil. Squeeze the garlic pulp into the tomato mixture. Add the onion and mushrooms and mix well. Reduce the heat and simmer for 15 minutes.

Spread 3/4 cup of the sauce evenly in an 8x8-inch baking dish. Layer one-half of the eggplant and one-half of the remaining sauce in the prepared dish. Spread a mixture of the ricotta cheese and Parmesan cheese over the sauce. Continue layering with the remaining eggplant and remaining sauce. Sprinkle with the mozzarella cheese. Bake at 375 degrees for 30 minutes.

Kristi Kimmell Casto

From Tailgates to Tree Stands

Grill & Game

My brothers and I all started hunting at an early age. One hunt, towards the end of the day,

my father brought me over about ten birds and told me to put them in my dove stool.

I did as I was told and didn't ask any questions. A little while later Kennedy, the game warden, showed up.

He went around checking all the hunters. When he got to me he saw I was hunting with a .410 shotgun.

He asked me how many birds I had in my stool and I told him fifteen. He looked rather surprised

and asked me if I had killed all those birds out of that dead pine tree. I told him no,

that my father had given about ten of his to me. I could hear my father laughing from across the field.

Hunting gear, tall tales, and tough lessons are important components of many family traditions.

—William Boon Bickerstaff

From Tailgates to Tree Stands

Grill & Game

Beef and Vegetable Skewers

Serves 6 to 8

1¹/2 pounds beef sirloin steak or tenderloin
1 green bell pepper
1 red bell pepper
1 yellow bell pepper
1 sweet onion or red onion
1 package fresh whole mushrooms

1 package fresh cherry tomatoes
1 (8-ounce) bottle lime juice
1 (4-ounce) bottle lemon juice
¹/2 cup olive oil
Salt and pepper to taste

Cut the steak into cubes. Cut the bell peppers and onion into squares. Divide the steak and vegetables into four equal portions so there will be equal amounts for each kabob. Thread each portion of the steak, onion, bell peppers, mushrooms and tomatoes alternately onto a skewer, using the colors of the bell peppers to complete a visually pleasing kabob. Mix the lime juice, lemon juice, olive oil, salt and pepper in an 8×11-inch glass baking dish. Add the kabobs. Marinate in the refrigerator for 6 to 18 hours, turning the kabobs halfway through the marinating time. Drain the kabobs, discarding the marinade. Place on a grill rack. Grill to the desired degree of doneness. Serve with hot cooked rice if desired.

Note: The longer you marinate these, the stronger the citrus flavor will be.

Kristi Kimmell Casto

Grilled Flank Steak

Serves 6 to 8

3 small to medium flank steaks
¹/2 cup soy sauce
¹/2 cup vegetable oil

1 tablespoon Worcestershire sauce
1 tablespoon A.1. steak sauce
3 garlic cloves

Place the steaks in a sealable plastic bag. Process the soy sauce, oil, Worcestershire sauce, A.1. sauce and garlic cloves in a blender until blended. Pour over the steaks and seal the bag. Marinate in the refrigerator for 3 hours. Drain the steak, discarding the marinade. Place the steak on a grill rack. Grill to medium-rare. Cut diagonally into slices and serve.

Lauren Brazil Briscoe

Wagyu Hanger Steak with Béarnaise Sauce

Serves 4

This is a must dish for those hard-to-impress dinner guests.

Steak	Béarnaise Sauce
2 Wagyu hanger steaks	2 egg yolks
Olive oil for rubbing	3 tablespoons fresh lemon juice
Coarse salt or kosher salt to taste	1/2 cup (1 stick) butter
Freshly cracked pepper to taste	1 tablespoon minced onion
	1 tablespoon chopped fresh tarragon
	2 tablespoons white wine

To prepare the steaks, pat the steaks dry and rub lightly with olive oil. Sprinkle with coarse salt and pepper. Sear in an ovenproof skillet over high heat to seal in the fat and the juices. Cook to 120 to 125 degrees on a meat thermometer. Bake at 350 degrees until a meat thermometer registers 130 degrees.

To prepare the sauce, beat the egg yolks and lemon juice briskly with a wooden spoon in a saucepan. Add one-half of the butter, the onion and tarragon. Heat over low heat until the butter is melted, stirring constantly. Add the remaining butter and the wine. Heat until the butter melts, stirring briskly. Serve over the steaks.

Gourmet Wagyu Steaks Internal Temperature Guide:
    Rare: 125 degrees to 130 degrees (USDA recommends 140 degrees)
    Medium-Rare: 130 degrees to 140 degrees (USDA recommends 150 degrees)
    Medium: 140 degrees to 150 degrees (USDA recommends 160 degrees)
    Medium-Well: 150 degrees to 160 degrees (USDA recommends 170 degrees)
    Well-Done: Not Recommended

Note: Due to their high fat content, it is best to sear
Wagyu hanger steaks at high temperature to seal in the fat and juices.
The steaks are best served rare to medium.

Joseph Carson Patrick

London Broil

Serves 6

1 1/2 pounds London broil	1 1/2 teaspoons ginger
5 green onions, chopped	3 tablespoons honey
3/4 cup vegetable oil	2 tablespoons vinegar
1/2 cup soy sauce	Salt and pepper to taste

Place the beef in a large sealable plastic bag. Mix the green onions, oil, soy sauce, ginger, honey, vinegar, salt and pepper in a bowl. Pour over the beef and seal the bag. Marinate in the refrigerator for 8 to 10 hours. Drain the beef, discarding the marinade. Place the beef on a grill rack. Grill over hot coals for 5 to 10 minutes on each side or to the desired degree of doneness.

Robin Alexander Grier

Stuffed Blue Cheese Burgers

Serves 4 or 5

4 ounces blue cheese, crumbled	1 1/2 tablespoons steak sauce
1/4 cup (1/2 stick) butter, softened	1 egg
1 pound ground chuck	1/2 teaspoon salt
8 ounces ground sirloin	1/4 teaspoon pepper
1/4 cup seasoned dry bread crumbs	4 or 5 hamburger buns

Mix the cheese and butter in a bowl. Chill for 1 hour. Shape into 4 or 5 balls and press into circles. Combine the ground chuck, ground sirloin, bread crumbs, steak sauce, egg, salt and pepper in a bowl and mix well. Shape into 4 or 5 patties. Press the cheese butter into the patties and shape the patties around the cheese butter to cover. Place on a grill rack. Grill until cooked through. Serve on the hamburger buns. Have lettuce, tomatoes and condiments ready for guests to serve themselves.

Michelle Moorman Cayes

Tailgate Burgers

Serves 3 or 4

1 pound lean ground beef	1/8 teaspoon pepper
1 egg	1 1/2 teaspoons minced onion
1 teaspoon Worcestershire sauce	2 tablespoons ketchup
1 teaspoon seasoned salt	3 or 4 hamburger buns
1/4 teaspoon salt	

Combine the ground beef, egg, Worcestershire sauce, seasoned salt, salt, pepper, onion and ketchup in a bowl and mix well. Shape into patties. Place on a grill rack. Grill until cooked through. Serve on the hamburger buns.

Sandy Tally Coolik

Butterflied Leg of Lamb with Wine

Serves 8

A butterflied leg of lamb is one that is boned and spread out flat.
This makes it cook more evenly, and it is easier to carve without the bone.

2/3 cup dry red wine	3 garlic cloves, minced
1/4 cup olive oil	1/2 teaspoon salt
5 tablespoons soy sauce	1/2 teaspoon pepper
1 1/2 tablespoons dried thyme	1 (6- to 7-pound) leg of lamb, trimmed of
1 1/2 tablespoons rosemary	excess fat, boned and butterflied
2 teaspoons grated lemon zest	

Whisk the wine, olive oil, soy sauce, thyme, rosemary, lemon zest, garlic, salt and pepper in a bowl. Place the lamb in a large sealable plastic bag and add the marinade. Press out the air and seal the bag tightly. Marinate in the refrigerator for 3 to 12 hours, turning occasionally.

Drain the lamb, reserving the marinade. Boil the reserved marinade in a saucepan and set aside. Pat the lamb dry with paper towels. Place on a grill rack. Grill to 145 degrees on a meat thermometer for medium-rare, turning several times and brushing with the boiled reserved marinade. Remove the lamb to a cutting board. Cover loosely with foil and let stand for 5 minutes. Carve into thin slices and serve.

Margie Thrasher Richardson

Pork Tenderloin

Serves 6 to 8

1/2 cup packed brown sugar	1 garlic clove, minced
1/2 cup Dijon mustard	2 teaspoons Worcestershire sauce
1/4 cup bourbon	Salt and pepper to taste
1/4 cup soy sauce	2 1/2 pounds pork tenderloin

Mix the brown sugar, Dijon mustard, bourbon, soy sauce, garlic, Worcestershire sauce, salt and pepper in a bowl. Place the pork in a sealable plastic bag. Add the marinade and seal the bag. Marinate in the refrigerator for 8 to 12 hours. Drain the pork, discarding the marinade. Place the pork on a grill rack. Grill, covered, for 45 to 60 minutes or to 160 degrees on a meat thermometer, turning occasionally. Remove the pork to a platter and cover with foil. Let stand for 10 minutes before serving.

Margaret Bradley McCormick

Fabulous Smoked Ribs

Serves 6

1 slab St. Louis-style or baby back ribs	1 cup (or more) packed brown sugar
1 (12-ounce) bottle Allegro hickory smoke marinade	1/2 (12-ounce) can Coca-Cola
Southern Flavor dry seasoning to taste	1 (18-ounce) bottle Sweet Baby Ray's barbecue sauce or your favorite
1 cup (or more) honey	barbecue sauce

Soak a bag of mesquite or hickory flavor wood chips in water; drain. Place the ribs in a sealable plastic bag. Add the marinade and seal the bag. Marinate in the refrigerator for 2 hours. Drain the ribs, discarding the marinade. Coat with the dry seasoning. Place on a rack over the wood chips in a smoker. Smoke at 275 to 300 degrees for 45 to 60 minutes. Coat a large sheet of foil with the honey and brown sugar. Place the ribs meat side down on the honey mixture. Wrap the ribs in the foil, leaving an opening in the top. Pour the Coca-Cola over the ribs and seal the top to completely enclose. Place on the smoker rack. Smoke at 275 to 300 degrees for 30 minutes. Remove the ribs from the foil and baste with the barbecue sauce. Place on the smoker rack. Smoke for 5 to 10 minutes and serve.

Jennings Adams DeWitt Palmer

Hickory Boston Butt

Serves 8 to 12

1 (3- to 4-pound) Boston butt
1 (12-ounce) bottle Allegro hickory smoke marinade
1¹/2 cups Southern Flavor dry seasoning

Place the pork in a sealable plastic bag. Add enough marinade to cover the pork and seal the bag. Marinate in the refrigerator for 8 to 12 hours, turning occasionally. Drain the pork, reserving the marinade. Coat the pork with the dry seasoning. Place on a rack over hickory or mesquite wood chips in a smoker. Smoke at 275 degrees for 7 to 8 hours, mopping with the reserved marinade frequently. Increase the heat to 350 to 375 degrees. Place the pork on a sheet of foil and pour the remaining marinade over the pork; seal tightly. Smoke for 2 to 3 hours or to 160 degrees on a meat thermometer. A larger Boston butt may require more than one bottle of Allegro.

Jennings Adams DeWitt Palmer

Buff's Chicken Monterey

Serves 4

1/2 cup soy sauce	2 bell peppers, sliced
1/2 cup Worcestershire sauce	6 mushrooms, sliced
2 tablespoons brown sugar	1/4 cup water
4 boneless chicken breasts	5 ounces Monterey Jack cheese, shredded
2 onions, sliced	

Mix the soy sauce, Worcestershire sauce and brown sugar in a 9×9-inch baking dish or baking pan. Add the chicken, turning to coat. Place the onions and bell peppers over the chicken. Scatter the mushrooms over the vegetables. Pour the water over the top.

There are three cooking options. The first recommendation is to use a Big Green Egg or other smoker. Place the baking dish on the grill rack and cook on medium heat for 20 minutes. Turn the chicken and cook for 20 minutes or until cooked through. Place the cheese on top of the chicken and cook until melted. The second option is a grill. Grill over medium heat for 20 minutes and turn the chicken. Grill for 15 minutes or until cooked through. Place the cheese on top of the chicken and grill until the cheese melts. Or third, bake, covered, at 300 degrees in a conventional oven for 30 minutes. Remove the cover and turn the chicken. Bake for 15 minutes or until cooked through. Top with the cheese and bake until the cheese melts.

Lunday Brooks Buffington

Grilled Lemon Chicken

Serves 6

1 chicken, cut up	1 garlic clove, crushed
1/2 cup dry white wine	1 teaspoon paprika
1/4 cup lemon juice	2 lemons, thinly sliced
2 tablespoons vegetable oil	Paprika for rolling

Place the chicken in a sealable plastic bag. Mix the wine, lemon juice, oil, garlic, 1 teaspoon paprika and one-half of the lemon slices in a bowl. Pour over the chicken and seal the bag. Marinate in the refrigerator for 3 hours. Drain the chicken, reserving the marinade. Place the chicken on a grill rack. Grill for 15 to 20 minutes. Turn the chicken. Grill for 20 to 40 minutes longer or until the chicken is cooked through, brushing with the reserved marinade. Roll the edges of the slices of 1 lemon in paprika and place around the chicken to garnish.

Jennifer Hartley Glover

Sweet-Heat Grilled Chicken

Serves 8 to 10

2 cups cider vinegar	1 teaspoon black pepper
1/4 cup packed dark brown sugar	3 tablespoons dried crushed red pepper
1/4 cup vegetable oil	8 to 10 bone-in chicken breasts
2 teaspoons salt	

Mix the vinegar, brown sugar, oil, salt, black pepper and red pepper in a bowl. Place one-half of the chicken and one-half of the marinade in each of two large sealable plastic bags and seal. Marinate for 2 to 8 hours, turning occasionally. (The chicken will become spicier the longer it marinates.) Drain the chicken, discarding the marinade. Place the chicken on a grill rack. Grill, covered with the grill lid, over medium-high heat (350 to 400 degrees) for 10 to 12 minutes on each side or until cooked through.

Note: Boneless chicken breasts can be used, but reduce the marinating and baking time by one-half.

Margaret Marston Ward

Grouper with Peach-Ginger Salsa

Serves 4

Peach-Ginger Salsa

2 cups chopped fresh or frozen peaches
1/2 cup chopped red bell pepper
1/3 cup rice wine vinegar
1/4 cup minced green onions
2 tablespoons minced fresh garlic
2 tablespoons sugar
1/2 teaspoon pepper
1/4 teaspoon salt
1/4 teaspoon hot pepper sauce
2 tablespoons fresh ginger, grated

Grouper

1 tablespoon chile paste or chile sauce with garlic, or to taste
4 grouper fillets

To prepare the salsa, combine the peaches, bell pepper, vinegar, green onions, garlic, sugar, pepper, salt, hot sauce and ginger in a bowl and mix well. Let stand for 1 hour.

To prepare the grouper, rub the chile paste on both sides of the fillets. (The more chile paste you use, the spicier it will be.) Place the fillets on a grill rack coated with nonstick cooking spray. Grill for 6 minutes on each side or until the fillets flake easily. Serve with the salsa and over hot cooked couscous, if desired.

Margaret Marston Ward

Cedar-Planked Salmon with Spicy Mustard Sauce

Serves 2

A divine recipe for a romantic night at home.

Spicy Mustard Sauce	Salmon
1 teaspoon butter, melted	2 salmon fillets
3/4 cup mayonnaise	1 tablespoon olive oil
2 tablespoons Dijon mustard	Salt and pepper to taste
1 teaspoon horseradish sauce	6 slices fresh lemon
Salt and freshly cracked pepper to taste	

To prepare the sauce, mix the butter and mayonnaise in a medium bowl. Add the Dijon mustard and horseradish sauce and mix well. Stir in salt and pepper. Chill for 1 hour or longer for the flavors to blend.

To prepare the salmon, soak cedar planks in water for 3 hours or longer. Remove from the water and set aside. Rub the fillets with the olive oil and place in a dish. Sprinkle with salt and pepper. Top with the lemon slices. Chill in the refrigerator until grilling time. Place the fillets on the cedar planks and place on a grill rack. Grill over medium-high heat for 15 to 20 minutes or until firm. Do not turn. Serve on the plank or remove to a serving plate. Drizzle the sauce over the top or serve on the side.

Mara Hall Kelly

I remember sitting in the rumble seat of my daddy's 1927 Pierce Arrow that previously belonged to Gloria Swanson, an actress in the 1930s. My daddy drove us through Averett Woods neighborhood past his elementary school and his high school. We would also pass the same duplex on Hilton where he lived in the 1940s, his mother lived in during the 1990s, and where I live today. Stories of Columbus were told galore during those special drives.

—Jennings Adams DeWitt Palmer

Bacon-Wrapped Venison

Serves 4 to 6

1 venison tenderloin	1/2 cup low-sodium Dale's steak seasoning
3 (12-ounce) cans beer	1 tablespoon fresh thyme, or 2 teaspoons
1 teaspoon salt	dried thyme
1/2 teaspoon pepper	1 pound thick-cut bacon

Place the venison in a large sealable plastic bag and add the beer. Marinate in the refrigerator for 2 to 4 hours. Drain the venison, discarding the marinade. Add the salt, pepper, steak seasoning and thyme. Marinate in the refrigerator for 2 to 4 hours or at room temperature for 1 to 2 hours. Drain the venison, discarding the marinade. Cut the venison into 1- to 2-inch slices or cubes. Wrap each with 1/2 to 1 slice of bacon and secure with wooden picks. Place on a grill rack. Grill for 6 to 8 minutes on each side or until done to taste.

Amelia Alcorn Vaught

Venison Jerky

Serves 4 to 6

1 venison roast	1 tablespoon minced garlic
1 cup soy sauce	1 teaspoon salt
1 cup teriyaki sauce	1 teaspoon pepper
1 cup packed brown sugar	1 teaspoon Tabasco sauce (optional)
1 tablespoon garlic powder	

Cut the venison into 1/4-inch-thick slices and place in a sealable plastic bag. Combine the soy sauce, teriyaki sauce, brown sugar, garlic powder, garlic, salt, pepper and Tabasco sauce in a bowl and mix well. Pour over the venison and seal the bag. Marinate in the refrigerator for 24 to 48 hours. Drain the venison, discarding the marinade. Place on a rack in a dehydrator. Dehydrate for 6 to 8 hours or until the venison bends but is not brittle.

Note: For Hot and Spicy Venison Jerky, purée 1 cup apple juice with 1 to 3 jalapeño chiles for mild, 1 to 3 chile peppers for medium or 1 habanero chile for very hot in a blender and add to the marinade before marinating the venison. The venison can also be dried in the oven set at the lowest temperature for 2 to 4 hours or until the venison bends but is not brittle.

Blakely Hanes Voltz

Buck and Bourbon Stew

Serves 6 to 8

2¹/2 pounds venison, cut into small cubes
5 tablespoons all-purpose flour
1 teaspoon salt
¹/4 teaspoon pepper
2¹/2 tablespoons vegetable oil
2 onions, chopped
1 cup chopped green bell pepper
2 garlic cloves, finely chopped

1 beef bouillon cube
1 cup water
2 potatoes, sliced
2 carrots, sliced
1 to 2 cups tomato sauce
¹/2 teaspoon thyme and/or
crushed rosemary
3 ounces bourbon

Shake the venison with the flour, salt and pepper in a sealable plastic bag to coat. Brown the venison in the oil in a large stockpot. Remove the venison and set aside. Add the onions, bell pepper and garlic to the pan drippings. Sauté until the vegetables are soft. Dissolve the bouillon cube in the water. Return the venison to the stockpot. Add the bouillon, potatoes, carrots, tomato sauce, thyme and bourbon and mix well. Simmer, covered, for 1¹/2 hours, adding additional liquid if needed.

Note: Substitute 1 cup beef broth for the bouillon cube and water, if desired.

Hugh Jefferson Bickerstaff, Jr.

"*N*early fell off my chair" means one was very surprised.

Venison Goulash

Serves 4 to 6

Chef Arceneaux delights the members of the Big Eddy Club with dishes such as this while portraying his creativity and commitment to fresh ingredients.

1/2 cup all-purpose flour
1 tablespoon sweet Hungarian paprika
1 sprig of fresh thyme, or 1/2 teaspoon thyme
1 teaspoon salt
1/2 teaspoon pepper
2 pounds boneless venison from hind quarters or foreleg,
cut into small bite-size cubes
5 tablespoons unsalted butter
2 onions, chopped
11/2 cups beef broth
2 large garlic cloves, minced
Salt to taste
10 large mushrooms, sliced
11/2 cups sour cream
Hot cooked rice or noodles

Mix the flour, paprika, thyme, 1 teaspoon salt and the pepper together in a shallow dish. Dredge the venison in the flour mixture. Sauté the venison in 3 tablespoons of the butter in a skillet until brown. Remove the venison from the skillet and set aside. Sauté the onions in the remaining 2 tablespoons butter and pan drippings until brown. Stir in the broth, garlic and salt to taste. Return the venison to the skillet. Cook, covered, for 30 minutes. Add the mushrooms. Stir in the sour cream. Cook over low heat for 7 to 10 minutes or until the venison is tender and juicy, stirring frequently. Serve over rice.

Eric Arceneaux

Savory Venison Pie

Serves 8 to 10

3 tablespoons sunflower oil
1 large onion, chopped
1 garlic clove, crushed
3 slices bacon, chopped
1 1/2 pounds ground venison
1 cup button mushrooms, chopped
2 tablespoons all-purpose flour
2 cups beef stock
2/3 cup ruby port
2 bay leaves
1 teaspoon thyme
1 teaspoon Dijon mustard
1 tablespoon red currant jelly
1/4 teaspoon salt, or more to taste

1/4 teaspoon freshly ground pepper, or
   more to taste
1 1/2 pounds potatoes, peeled and
   cut into chunks
1 pound parsnips, peeled and cut into
   large chunks
Salt to taste
1 egg yolk
1/4 cup (1/2 stick) butter
3 tablespoons chopped parsley
1/4 teaspoon nutmeg, or more to taste
Pepper to taste
2 unbaked (9-inch) pie shells

Heat the sunflower oil in a large skillet. Add the onion, garlic and bacon. Cook for 5 minutes, stirring frequently. Add the venison and mushrooms. Cook for 3 minutes or until brown, stirring until crumbly. Stir in the flour. Cook for 1 to 2 minutes. Add the stock, wine, bay leaves, thyme, Dijon mustard, jelly, 1/4 teaspoon salt and 1/4 teaspoon pepper. Bring to a boil and reduce the heat. Simmer, covered, for 30 to 40 minutes or until tender. Discard the bay leaves.

Cook the potatoes and parsnips in boiling salted water in a saucepan for 20 minutes or until tender. Drain and mash. Beat in the egg yolk, butter, parsley, nutmeg, salt and pepper to taste. Spoon the venison mixture into the pie shells, leveling the surface. Spread the potato mixture over the top. Bake at 325 degrees for 30 to 40 minutes or until golden brown. Serve immediately.

Merle Cauthen Morgan, Seale, Alabama

"It's a sure sign of summer if the chair gets up when you do."

— *Walter Winchell*

Boon's Dove

Serves 2 to 4

1/4 cup (1/2 stick) butter	4 sprigs each of fresh parsley and thyme or
8 dove	rosemary, chopped
Salt and pepper to taste	1 tablespoon all-purpose flour
1 (3-ounce) jar sliced button mushrooms	2 cups chicken broth or game bird stock
1/2 cup chopped onion	1/2 cup dry sherry

Melt the butter in a skillet. Add the birds. Cook until brown on all sides. Sprinkle lightly with salt and pepper. Place the birds in a baking dish. Drain the mushrooms, reserving the juice. Add the onion, parsley, thyme and mushrooms to the pan drippings. Cook for 5 minutes or until brown. Add the flour. Cook until brown and bubbly, stirring constantly. Reduce the heat. Add the broth and reserved mushroom liquid. Cook until smooth, stirring constantly. Add the sherry. Simmer for 1 minute. Adjust the seasonings to taste. Pour over the birds. Bake, covered, at 325 degrees for 1 1/2 hours or until the birds are tender.

William Boon Bickerstaff

Dove in Wine Sauce

Serves 6 to 8

16 dove	1/4 teaspoon sugar
Salt and pepper to taste	1/4 cup mustard
1/2 cup (1 stick) butter	1 cup (or more) burgundy
1/2 cup ketchup	1 teaspoon salt
1/4 cup Worcestershire sauce	1/4 teaspoon pepper
2 tablespoons lemon juice	Hot cooked rice

Sprinkle the birds with salt and pepper to taste. Melt the butter in a skillet over medium-high heat. Add the birds and cook until brown. Reduce the heat to low. Add enough hot water to cover. Cook, covered, for 2 hours or until tender.

Drain the birds. Mix the ketchup, Worcestershire sauce, lemon juice, sugar, mustard, wine, 1 teaspoon salt and 1/4 teaspoon pepper in a bowl. Pour over the birds. Cook for 1 hour or until very tender, adding additional wine if the sauce becomes too thick. Serve over rice.

Nell Higdon Hudson

Grilled Duck with Juniper Berries

Serves 4

Mitchell Jarrett has not traveled far from his hometown of Columbus to open Mama's Boy in Athens, Georgia, voted best breakfast by the Athens Banner Herald. This recipe pairs well with Wild and Brown Rice Baked with Apricots on page 129.

2 to 4 medium boneless duck breasts
(about 8 ounces each)
3 tablespoons extra-virgin olive oil
2 tablespoons dark soy sauce
Juice and zest of 3 lemons
20 juniper berries, ground
Pinch each of salt and pepper

Place the duck breasts in a sealable plastic bag. Mix the olive oil, soy sauce, lemon juice, lemon zest, juniper berries, salt and pepper in a bowl. Pour over the duck breasts and seal the bag. Marinate in the refrigerator for 3 hours or longer. Drain the duck breasts, discarding the marinade. Place the duck breasts on a grill rack. Grill over medium heat for 10 to 20 minutes on each side or until cooked through.

Note: The juniper berries can be ground in a coffee grinder, in a mortar with a pestle, or crushed with the flat part of a knife and then finely chopped.

Mitchell Jarett, Athens, Georgia

My first day of law school, first class, and the only chair available was next to my future husband. How lucky can you get?

— April Halstead Hocutt

Spicy Duck Wrap

Serves 1

1 duck breast fillet	5 or 6 slices jalapeño chile
1 cup olive oil	1/2 slice bacon
1 chunk Monterey Jack cheese	Salt and pepper to taste

Place the duck breast in a sealable plastic bag. Add the olive oil and seal the bag. Marinate in the refrigerator for 3 hours. Drain the duck breast, discarding the olive oil. Cut a pocket in the middle of the duck breast and fill with the cheese and jalapeño chile slices. Wrap with the bacon and secure with a wooden pick. Sprinkle with salt and pepper. Place on a grill rack. Grill for 2 to 3 minutes on each side or until the bacon is cooked through. Do not overcook the duck.

Blakely Hanes Voltz

Buttermilk Fried Quail

Serves 2

Serve with mashed potatoes or grits for a truly Southern meal.

4 quail breasts	1/2 teaspoon pepper
3 cups (or more) buttermilk	Vegetable oil for frying
1 cup white cornmeal	11/2 to 2 tablespoons all-purpose flour
1 cup all-purpose flour	Pinch of salt
1/2 to 1 teaspoon salt	1/2 to 3/4 cup water

Marinate the quail breasts in buttermilk to cover in a bowl in the refrigerator for 30 to 60 minutes. Place the cornmeal, 1 cup flour, 1/2 to 1 teaspoon salt and the pepper in a bag and shake to mix well. Add the quail breasts and shake to coat. Pour 1/2 inch oil into a skillet and heat to 375 degrees. Add the quail breasts and fry until brown and cooked through. Remove to paper towels to drain.

Drain the skillet, reserving 1/3 cup of the drippings in the skillet. Stir in 11/2 to 2 tablespoons flour and a pinch of salt. Cook until light brown, stirring constantly. Add the water gradually and cook to the desired consistency, stirring constantly. Reduce the heat once the gravy is the desired consistency. Serve over the quail breasts.

Note: A mixture of vegetable oil and olive oil can be used for frying.

Timothy George Gregory, Jr.

Hearty Braised Quail

Serves 2

6 quail, skinned	2 garlic cloves, minced
1/2 teaspoon coarse salt	1/2 cup dry white wine such as chablis
1/4 teaspoon pepper	1/4 teaspoon dried whole thyme
1 cup fresh button mushrooms, sliced	2 tomatoes, cut into wedges
4 green onions, sliced	1 tablespoon chopped fresh parsley

Rinse the quail under cold water and pat dry. Sprinkle with the coarse salt and pepper. Coat a skillet generously with nonstick cooking spray and heat over medium-high heat. Add the quail. Cook until light brown on each side. Drain and pat dry. Set the quail aside. Wipe the skillet clean.

Coat the skillet with nonstick cooking spray. Add the mushrooms. Sauté over medium-high heat for 3 to 4 minutes or until tender. Remove the mushrooms and set aside. Wipe the skillet clean.

Coat the skillet with nonstick cooking spray. Add the green onions and garlic. Sauté over medium-high heat for 1 minute. Stir in the wine and thyme. Return the quail to the skillet and bring the liquid to a boil. Cover and reduce the heat. Simmer for 25 minutes. Add the mushrooms and tomatoes. Cover and simmer for 4 minutes. Spoon into a serving dish and sprinkle with the parsley.

Hadley Upchurch Scott

Smothered Quail

Serves 2

2 cups baking mix	11/2 cups (about) shortening
1/2 teaspoon salt	2 tablespoons baking mix
1/2 teaspoon pepper	2 cups (or more) water
4 quail	

Mix 2 cups baking mix, the salt and pepper in a nonrecycled paper bag. Add the quail two at a time and shake to coat. Melt enough shortening in an electric skillet to fill 1/2 inch. Place the quail cavity side down in the hot shortening. Fry, covered, until brown. Turn and fry until brown. Remove the quail and set aside. Drain the skillet, leaving 6 tablespoons of the drippings in the skillet. Stir in 2 tablespoons baking mix. Cook until brown, stirring constantly. Return the quail to the skillet. Add the water. Reduce the heat. Simmer until the quail are tender and the gravy is thickened, adding additional water for the desired consistency if needed.

Edith Harwell McCullough

Quail with White Sauce

Serves 2

6 quail breasts	1 1/2 cups (or more) milk
2 tablespoons butter	1/2 teaspoon garlic salt
1 onion, chopped	Salt and pepper to taste
1/2 cup mushrooms, chopped or sliced	1 teaspoon Kitchen Bouquet or other
1/2 cup finely chopped celery	gravy sauce
1/4 cup finely chopped red bell pepper	1 cup sour cream
2 tablespoons all-purpose flour	

Arrange the quail in a baking dish. Melt the butter in a skillet. Add the onion, mushrooms, celery and bell pepper and sauté until tender. Stir in the flour. Add the milk gradually. Cook until thickened, stirring constantly. Stir in the garlic salt, salt, pepper and Kitchen Bouquet. Pour over the quail. Bake, covered, at 350 degrees for 20 minutes. Remove 1/2 cup of the sauce and mix with the sour cream in a bowl. Continue to bake the quail, uncovered, for 20 minutes. Serve with the cream sauce.

Gardiner Zollo Church

Grilled Fillet of Pheasant

Serves 4

6 pheasant fillets	1 jalapeño chile, seeded and chopped
1 (8-ounce) bottle Italian salad dressing	1 small onion, chopped
8 ounces whipped cream cheese	6 slices bacon

Place the fillets in a sealable plastic bag. Add the salad dressing and seal the bag. Marinate in the refrigerator for 2 hours. Drain the fillets, discarding the marinade. Spread each fillet with the cream cheese. Top with the jalapeño chile and onion and roll up. Wrap each fillet with a slice of bacon and secure with a wooden pick. Place on a grill rack. Grill over medium heat for 7 minutes. This is delicious served with wild rice and asparagus.

Jennings Adams DeWitt Palmer

Pheasant Roast with Port

Serves 4

2 (1- to 2-pound) pheasant
1/4 cup (1/2 stick) butter, softened
8 sprigs of fresh thyme
2 bay leaves
6 slices bacon
1/4 teaspoon salt, or to taste
1 teaspoon freshly ground pepper, or to taste
1 tablespoon all-purpose flour
1/4 cup game stock or chicken stock, plus more if needed
1 tablespoon red currant jelly
1/4 cup good-quality port

Line a large roasting pan with a sheet of heavy-duty foil large enough to enclose the pheasant. Brush the foil lightly with vegetable oil or spray with nonstick cooking spray. Wipe the pheasant with damp paper towels and remove any extra fat or skin. Loosen the skin of the breasts using your fingertips. Spread the butter between the skin and breast of each pheasant. Tie the legs securely with string. Lay the thyme sprigs and a bay leaf over each breast. Lay the bacon over the top of each. Place in the prepared pan. Sprinkle with the salt and pepper. Bring up the foil and fold to securely enclose the pheasant. Roast at 450 degrees for 20 minutes. Reduce the oven temperature to 375 degrees. Roast for 40 minutes. Uncover and roast for 10 to 15 minutes longer or until golden brown. Remove the birds to a carving board and let stand for 10 minutes before carving.

Pour the pan juices into the roasting pan and skim the fat. Sprinkle with the flour. Cook over medium heat until smooth, stirring constantly. Whisk in the stock and jelly. Bring to a boil and reduce the heat. Simmer until thickened slightly, stirring constantly. Stir in the wine and adjust the seasonings. Serve with the pheasant.

Merle Cauthen Morgan

Grilled Asparagus with Prosciutto

Serves 4

The use of the vegetable grill pan is highly recommended as it prevents the asparagus from falling through the grates. If a grill pan is unavailable, the asparagus can be threaded onto wooden skewers. Be sure to wrap the exposed ends of the skewers in little pieces of foil to prevent charring.

2 pounds fresh asparagus, trimmed
2 or 3 tablespoons extra-virgin olive oil
Kosher salt and pepper to taste

6 thinly shaved slices prosciutto
1/2 cup (2 ounces) finely grated
Parmigiano-Reggiano cheese

Toss the asparagus with the olive oil in a shallow dish. Sprinkle with kosher salt and pepper. Heat a vegetable grill pan on a grill rack over medium-high heat for 2 minutes. Place the asparagus in the hot pan. Grill for 8 to 10 minutes or until tender, turning occasionally. Place the prosciutto on the grill rack. Grill for 3 to 4 minutes or until crisp. Place the asparagus on a serving dish and crumble the prosciutto over the top. Sprinkle with the cheese. Serve immediately.

Hadley Upchurch Scott

Grilled Rosemary Corn

Serves 6

6 ears of fresh yellow corn with stalks
6 tablespoons butter

6 sprigs of fresh rosemary
Salt and pepper to taste

Pull back the husks, leaving them attached to the bases. Remove the silks. Reposition the husks. Soak in a sink or bowl of cold water for 10 minutes or longer. Remove from the water and gently pull back one side of the husks. Place 1 tablespoon butter, one sprig of rosemary and salt and pepper on each ear of corn. Reposition the husks. Place on a grill rack. Grill over indirect heat for 40 minutes or until tender.

Julie Davenport Davis

Grilled Portobello Mushrooms with Spinach and Gouda

Serves 4

1 small shallot, finely chopped	2 tablespoons olive oil
1/4 cup Champagne vinegar or red vinegar	1 teaspoon salt
2 1/2 teaspoons Dijon mustard	1 teaspoon freshly ground pepper
1/4 teaspoon salt	8 ounces baby spinach
1/4 teaspoon freshly ground pepper	2 ounces Gouda cheese, thinly sliced
1 garlic clove, minced	2 tablespoons finely chopped fresh
1/4 cup olive oil	parsley, for garnish
8 portobello mushroom caps	

Whisk the shallot, vinegar, Dijon mustard, 1/4 teaspoon salt, 1/4 teaspoon pepper and the garlic in a bowl. Whisk in 1/4 cup olive oil and set aside.

Brush the mushroom caps on both sides with 2 tablespoons olive oil. Sprinkle with 1 teaspoon salt and 1 teaspoon pepper. Place cap side down on a grill rack. Grill for 3 to 4 minutes or until slightly charred. Turn the mushroom caps over. Grill for 3 to 4 minutes longer or until cooked through.

Toss the spinach with some of the vinaigrette in a bowl. For each serving, layer some of the spinach, some of the cheese and a mushroom cap on a serving plate. Repeat in the same order, ending with a mushroom cap. Drizzle the remaining vinaigrette over each serving and garnish with the parsley.

Nell Louise Taylor, Columbus, Mississippi

Balsamic Grilled Vegetables

Serves 6 to 8

1/4 cup balsamic vinegar	4 Roma tomatoes, cut into halves
2 tablespoons honey	1 red bell pepper, cut into 8 wedges
1 tablespoon olive oil	1 onion, cut into wedges 2 inches thick
1 teaspoon coarsely ground pepper	1 each zucchini and yellow squash,
1/2 teaspoon salt	cut lengthwise into slices 1 inch thick
4 garlic cloves, minced	

Mix the vinegar, honey, olive oil, pepper, salt and garlic in a bowl. Combine the vegetables in a bowl and toss to mix. Divide the vegetables and vinegar mixture evenly between two large sealable plastic bags; seal the bags. Marinate in the refrigerator for 1 hour. Drain the vegetables, reserving the marinade. Place the vegetables in a grill basket coated with nonstick cooking spray. Grill over medium-high heat for 10 to 14 minutes or until the onion is tender, stirring occasionally and basting with the reserved marinade.

Margaret Marston Ward

"*Nature is by and large to be found out of doors, a location where, it cannot be argued, there are never enough comfortable chairs.*"

— *Fran Lebowitz*

Finishing Sauce

Makes 3 cups

*Enjoy the culinary expertise of well-known South Georgia
resident Bryan Hardegree. As a competition barbecue chef, he delights
in sticky fingers and saucy smiles.*

4 cups barbecue sauce
1/2 cup peach preserves or
apricot preserves
1/2 cup honey
Minced garlic to taste
Tabasco sauce to taste

Combine the barbecue sauce, preserves and honey in a saucepan and mix well. Bring to a boil, stirring constantly. Stir in the garlic and Tabasco sauce. Any other spices can be added, if desired. Remove from the heat. Apply to the meat during the last 30 to 60 minutes of cooking time.

William Bryan Hardegree, Jr.

Basic Barbecue Sauce

Serves 20

A delicious accompaniment to chicken, pork, and turkey.

1 1/2 cups ketchup
1 tablespoon mustard
3 tablespoons Worcestershire sauce
1 tablespoon garlic salt
1 tablespoon Tabasco sauce
1/2 cup vinegar
1/2 cup packed brown sugar

Combine the ketchup, mustard, Worcestershire sauce, garlic salt, Tabasco sauce, vinegar and brown sugar in a bowl and mix well. Pour into an airtight container and store in the refrigerator.

Mallory Perkins Harris

Citrus Barbecue Sauce

Serves 15

To give as a gift, pour the sauce into individual Mason jars.

3 cups ketchup
2 cups packed dark brown sugar
1/2 cup cane syrup
1/2 cup lime juice
1/2 cup lemon juice
1/2 cup grapefruit juice
3/4 cup mango nectar
3/4 cup passion fruit juice or passion fruit juice cocktail
3/4 cup orange juice
1 1/2 tablespoons dry mustard
1 teaspoon onion powder
1 1/2 teaspoons white pepper
1/2 teaspoon red pepper
1/2 teaspoon kosher salt
1/2 teaspoon ground cumin
3 tablespoons cornstarch
2 tablespoons (about) water

Combine the ketchup, brown sugar, cane syrup, lime juice, lemon juice, grapefruit juice, mango nectar, passion fruit juice, orange juice, dry mustard, onion powder, white pepper, red pepper, kosher salt and cumin in a large bowl and mix well. Mix the cornstarch with just enough of the water to dissolve. Pour the sauce into a Dutch oven. Stir in the dissolved cornstarch. Cook over low heat until the sauce is the consistency of a thick syrup. Remove from the heat. Let stand, uncovered, until cool. Pour into sealable jars. Use as a marinade, basting sauce or table sauce.

Anne Hayes Drinkard Pearce

Molasses Barbecue Sauce

Makes 3 cups

The perfect accompaniment to ribs, chicken, or beef.

2 tablespoons olive oil
1 small onion, chopped
4 garlic cloves, minced
1 teaspoon red pepper flakes
1 tablespoon dry mustard
1/3 cup Worcestershire sauce

1/3 cup apple cider vinegar
1/4 cup unsulphured molasses
1/4 cup packed dark brown sugar
1/4 teaspoon pepper
2 cups ketchup

Heat the olive oil in a medium saucepan over medium heat. Add the onion and garlic. Cook for 5 minutes or until the mixture is translucent, stirring constantly. Stir in the red pepper flakes and dry mustard. Cook for 1 minute. Reduce the heat to medium-low. Stir in the Worcestershire sauce, vinegar, molasses, brown sugar, pepper and ketchup. Simmer for 10 minutes or until thickened, stirring occasionally. Remove from the heat to cool completely. Spoon into airtight containers and store in the refrigerator.

Hadley Upchurch Scott

Beef Marinade

Serves 6 to 8

4 garlic cloves
2 to 3 teaspoons Accent
2 teaspoons ground cumin
1 1/2 teaspoons smoke-flavored hickory salt
1 tablespoon salt

1 teaspoon pepper
4 or 5 drops of Tabasco sauce
1 cup yellow mustard
1 to 1 1/2 cups olive oil or canola oil

Process the garlic, Accent, cumin, hickory salt, salt, pepper, Tabasco sauce, mustard and olive oil in a blender until blended. Use to marinate beef in the refrigerator for 2 to 4 hours. It is an excellent marinade to use when grilling for company.

Shelly Mathews Blanton

Spicy Injection Marinade

Makes 6 cups

1 (32-ounce) jar apple juice
1 (14-ounce) can chicken broth
1/4 cup garlic powder
1/4 cup onion powder
2 tablespoons celery salt
2 tablespoons salt
2 tablespoons red pepper

Process the apple juice, broth, garlic powder, onion powder, celery salt, salt and red pepper in a blender. Chill, covered, for 8 to 10 hours. While injecting, keep the container stirred to prevent settling. This is a good injection for pork, beef, chicken and turkey. Always keep the needle moving while injecting to avoid having a pocket of spices.

William Bryan Hardegree, Jr.

Teriyaki Marinade

Makes about 2 3/4 cups

3/4 cup olive oil
1/2 cup soy sauce
1/2 cup honey
1 1/2 teaspoons fresh ginger
2 garlic cloves
1 cup chopped green onions

Combine the olive oil, soy sauce, honey, ginger, garlic and green onions in a bowl and mix well. Use to marinate up to 5 pounds of beef or chicken for as long as possible.

Jennifer Corradino Flournoy

From Rockers to Recliners

Desserts & Sweets

Several years ago, my father Cecil Cheves, went to Pennsylvania with the goal of
returning with a slab of English walnut that was large enough to make five rocking chairs...
two for he and my mother, Bettye, and one for me and my two sisters. With the help of his friend and
woodworker, Charles Brock, the vision has become a reality, and each of us has our own rocking chair,
lovingly handcrafted by our father along with a personalized carved message under each seat.
The story for this new heirloom is yet to be written.

— Olivia Cheves Blanchard

From Rockers to Recliners

Desserts & Sweets

Peach Ginger Crème Brûlée

Serves 6

8 ounces peaches, puréed
2 cups heavy cream
1/2 cup sugar
1/2 teaspoon ginger
1 1/4 cups egg yolks (about 16 large egg yolks)
1/2 cup sugar
1/2 teaspoon vanilla extract
Sugar for sprinkling

Bring the peaches, cream, 1/2 cup sugar and the ginger to a boil in a saucepan over medium heat, stirring frequently. Combine the egg yolks, 1/2 cup sugar and the vanilla in a bowl and mix well. Stir a small amount of the hot peach mixture into the egg yolk mixture; then stir the egg yolk mixture into the peach mixture. Strain through a wire mesh strainer into a bowl. Pour into individual ramekins, filling two-thirds full. Place the ramekins in a large baking pan. Add enough water to the baking pan to come halfway up the side of the ramekins. Bake at 250 degrees for 1 1/2 hours. Remove from the oven and cool completely in the water bath. Remove the ramekins from the water bath. Chill for 2 to 3 hours.

Just before serving, sprinkle a small amount of sugar on top of each crème brûlée. Broil until the sugar caramelizes and turns light brown.

Note: The water bath heats and cooks the crème brûlée gently. This is especially important for flan, custards, sauces, and mousses to prevent curdling.

Elvis (Kip) Hammersley, Jr.

Lemon Biscotti Cheesecake

Serves 10 to 12

10 to 12 ounces biscotti
6 tablespoons unsalted butter, melted
10 ounces whole milk ricotta cheese
12 ounces cream cheese, softened
2 cups sugar

5 eggs
1 1/2 cups sour cream
2 tablespoons grated lemon zest
3 tablespoons fresh lemon juice

Process the biscotti in a food processor until finely ground. Add the butter gradually, pulsing until moistened. Spread evenly in a 9-inch springform pan and press down. Bake at 350 degrees for 15 minutes or until golden brown. Remove from the oven and cool completely on a wire rack. Wrap the bottom and side in two layers of foil. Maintain the oven temperature.

Beat the ricotta cheese in a mixing bowl until smooth. Add the cream cheese and beat until smooth. Beat in the sugar, stopping occasionally to scrape the side of the bowl. Add the eggs one at a time, beating well after each addition. Add the sour cream, lemon zest and lemon juice and mix well. Pour into the cooled crust, leaving 1/4 inch from the top of the filling to the top of the pan. Place in a large baking pan. Fill the baking pan with enough hot water to come halfway up the side of the springform pan. Bake for 1 hour and 25 minutes or until the filling is slightly puffy and moves slightly when shaken. Remove from the water bath and cool for 2 hours. Chill in the refrigerator.

Joseph Carson Patrick

Cream Cheese Delights

Serves 12

12 vanilla wafers
16 ounces cream cheese, softened
1 cup sugar
2 eggs, beaten

1 teaspoon vanilla extract
1 (21-ounce) can blueberry pie filling or
   strawberry pie filling

Line twelve muffin cups with paper liners. Place a vanilla wafer in the bottom of each. Beat the cream cheese and sugar in a mixing bowl until smooth and creamy. Add the eggs and vanilla and beat well. Pour evenly into the prepared muffin cups. Bake at 350 degrees for 20 minutes. Top with the pie filling.

Shelly Mathews Blanton

Georgia Peach Cobbler

Serves 6 to 8

8 or 9 small peaches, peeled and thinly sliced
5 slices soft white bread, crusts trimmed
1¼ cups sugar

2 tablespoons all-purpose flour
1 egg, lightly beaten
½ cup (1 stick) butter, melted
1 teaspoon light brown sugar for garnish

Place the peaches in an 8-inch baking dish sprayed with nonstick cooking spray. Cut each slice of bread into five long strips. Place over the peaches. Combine the sugar, flour, egg and butter in a small bowl and mix well. Pour over the bread. Bake at 350 degrees for 30 minutes or until golden brown. Garnish with the brown sugar.

Eleanor Glenn Hardegree

Fruit Crisp

Serves 8

6 tablespoons all-purpose flour
¼ cup packed light brown sugar
¼ cup granulated sugar
¼ teaspoon cinnamon
¼ teaspoon nutmeg
¼ teaspoon salt
5 tablespoons unsalted butter, cut into ½-inch pieces

¾ cup chopped pecans
6 cups fruit (see note)
⅓ cup granulated sugar
1½ tablespoons lemon juice
½ teaspoon grated lemon zest
Vanilla ice cream

Pulse the flour, brown sugar, ¼ cup granulated sugar, the cinnamon, nutmeg, salt and butter five times in 3-second bursts until of a coarse cornmeal texture. Add the pecans and pulse five times in 1-second bursts. Chill in the refrigerator. Toss the fruit with ⅓ cup granulated sugar, the lemon juice and lemon zest in a bowl. Place in an 8×8-inch baking pan or 9-inch deep-dish pie plate. Spread the pecan mixture evenly over the top. Bake at 375 degrees for 40 minutes. Increase the oven temperature to 400 degrees. Bake for 5 minutes longer. Serve warm with ice cream.

Note: Try using 5 cups sliced peaches and 1 cup blueberries, pears or plums. If you use blueberries or plums, add 1 tablespoon tapioca.

Eleanor Glenn Hardegree

Sour Cream Banana Pudding

Serves 6

1 (4-ounce) package vanilla instant pudding mix	1 cup sour cream
	1 teaspoon butter flavoring
1 (4-ounce) package banana cream instant pudding mix	8 ounces whipped topping
	1 (12-ounce) package vanilla wafers
1 1/2 cups milk	6 bananas, chopped

Combine the vanilla pudding mix, banana cream pudding mix and milk in a mixing bowl and beat until thick. Add the sour cream and butter flavoring and beat well. Beat in the whipped topping. Alternate layers of the vanilla wafers, bananas and pudding mixture in a trifle bowl until all ingredients are used, ending with the pudding mixture. Chill for 1 hour or longer before serving.

Amy Giuliano Adams

Bourbon Bread Pudding

Serves 10

2 tablespoons butter	1 1/4 teaspoons cinnamon
1 loaf French bread	1 1/4 cups raisins
1 quart 2% milk	5 tablespoons butter
2 eggs, beaten	3/4 cup sugar
1 1/2 cups sugar	1 egg
2 tablespoons vanilla extract	1/4 cup bourbon

Coat the bottom and sides of a 9×13-inch baking dish with 2 tablespoons butter. Tear the bread into small pieces and place in a bowl. Add the milk. Let stand until most of the milk is absorbed. Add 2 eggs, 1 1/2 cups sugar, the vanilla, cinnamon and raisins and mix well. Pour into the prepared baking dish. Bake at 375 degrees for 1 hour.

Melt 5 tablespoons butter with 3/4 cup sugar in a double boiler over hot water. Whisk in the egg gradually. Whisk in the bourbon. Cook until thickened, whisking constantly. Pour over the pudding and serve, or serve warm on the side.

Edie Pendleton Evans

Sweet Surprise

Serves 8

3 egg whites	10 saltine crackers, crushed
Pinch of salt	1 teaspoon vanilla extract
1/2 teaspoon cream of tartar	Whipped cream
1 cup sugar	Fresh strawberries
1/2 cup chopped pecans	

Beat the egg whites in a mixing bowl until foamy. Add the salt and cream of tartar and beat until soft peaks form. Beat in the sugar gradually until stiff peaks form. Fold in the pecans, cracker crumbs and vanilla. Pour into a buttered 8×8-inch baking dish. Bake at 300 degrees for 30 minutes. Remove from the oven and cool slightly. Cut into squares. Serve topped with whipped cream and fresh strawberries.

Teresa Carswell Howard

Roasted Pears with Candied Hazelnuts and Syrup

Serves 6

1 cup water	6 large Bosc pears with stems, rinsed
1 1/4 cups sugar	3 tablespoons Frangelico
1 cup hazelnuts, coarsely chopped	2 tablespoons lemon juice
1 1/2 tablespoons unsalted butter	1 teaspoon vanilla extract

Simmer the water and 1 1/4 cups sugar in a saucepan until the sugar dissolves. Add the hazelnuts. Cook for 1 minute. Drain the hazelnuts, reserving the syrup. Spread the hazelnuts in a buttered baking pan. Bake at 325 degrees for 10 to 15 minutes or until golden brown. Add 1 1/2 tablespoons butter and toss until melted. Separate the hazelnuts and let stand until cool. The syrup and candied hazelnuts may be prepared up to 2 days in advance and stored separately in airtight containers. Increase the oven temperature to 350 degrees.

Dip the unpeeled pears into the reserved syrup. Stand upright in a buttered 2-quart baking pan. Sprinkle with additional sugar. Stir the liqueur, lemon juice and vanilla into the remaining reserved syrup. Pour into the baking pan. Roast on the middle oven rack for 30 minutes. Place the pears on serving plates. Spoon the syrup around the pears and sprinkle with the candied hazelnuts.

Joannie Siano Minter

Tiramisu

Serves 6 to 8

6 egg yolks	3/4 cup strong brewed coffee,
3/4 cup sugar	at room temperature
2/3 cup milk	6 tablespoons Kahlúa
1 pound mascarpone cheese	2 (7-ounce) packages ladyfingers
1 1/4 cups heavy whipping cream	1 tablespoon baking cocoa
1/2 teaspoon vanilla extract	

Whisk the egg yolks and sugar in a medium saucepan until blended. Whisk in the milk. Bring to a boil over medium heat, stirring constantly. Boil gently for 1 minute. Remove from the heat and cool slightly. Chill, tightly covered, for 1 hour. Add the cheese and beat with an electric mixer fitted with a whisk until smooth.

Beat the cream with the vanilla in a mixing bowl until firm peaks form. Mix the coffee and liqueur in a small bowl. Split the ladyfingers into halves lengthwise. Drizzle with the coffee mixture. Arrange one-half of the soaked ladyfingers in the bottom of a 7×11-inch glass dish. Spread with half the cheese mixture and half the whipped cream. Repeat the layers. Sprinkle with the baking cocoa. Chill, covered, for 24 to 48 hours. Cut into squares and serve cold.

Katie Taylor Coakley

Grandmother Tennant's Icebox Cake

Serves 12

1 cup (2 sticks) butter, softened	6 egg yolks
2 cups sugar	6 egg whites, stiffly beaten
4 ounces unsweetened chocolate	1 (12-ounce) package vanilla wafers,
1/2 cup hot water	coarsely crumbled

Cream the butter in a mixing bowl. Add the sugar and beat until light and fluffy. Dissolve the chocolate in the hot water. Beat the egg yolks in a mixing bowl until light. Add to the butter mixture and mix well. Add the chocolate mixture and mix well. Fold in the egg whites.

Spread a 1/4-inch layer of vanilla wafer crumbs in an 8×8-inch baking dish. Layer the chocolate mixture, the remaining vanilla wafer crumbs and the remaining chocolate mixture over the vanilla wafer crumb layer. Chill for 24 hours or until set.

Note: If you are concerned about using raw eggs, use eggs pasteurized in their shells, which are sold at some specialty food stores, or use an equivalent amount of pasteurized egg substitute.

Erwin Davidson Key

Coffee Ice Cream Cake

Serves 6 to 8

28 chocolate sandwich cookies, crushed	Dash of salt
3 tablespoons butter	3/4 cup sugar
1/2 gallon coffee ice cream, softened	2/3 cup cream or evaporated milk
3 ounces unsweetened chocolate	1/2 cup pecans or walnuts, toasted
3 tablespoons butter	and chopped

Process the cookie crumbs and 3 tablespoons butter in a food processor or blender until well mixed. Press firmly into a 9×13-inch dish. Freeze for 45 minutes or until firm. Spread the ice cream over the frozen layer. Freeze until firm.

Melt the chocolate, 3 tablespoons butter, dash of salt and the sugar in a saucepan over low heat. Stir in the cream gradually, watching carefully to prevent burning. Remove from the heat to cool. Spread over the frozen ice cream layer. Sprinkle with the pecans. Store in the freezer. The pecans can be lightly sautéed in butter.

Gardiner Zollo Church

Chocolate Ice Cream

Serves 12

4 ounces unsweetened chocolate
2 cups sugar
4 eggs
Dash of salt
1 quart milk
1 tablespoon vanilla extract
1 1/2 teaspoons cinnamon
1 quart cream

Melt the chocolate in a large saucepan over low heat. Melt the sugar with the eggs and salt in a saucepan over low heat, stirring constantly. Add to the melted chocolate and mix well. Add the milk. Cook over low heat for 3 to 5 minutes or until smooth, stirring frequently. Add the vanilla, cinnamon and cream. Allow the mixture to curdle slightly, but do not boil. Cool in the refrigerator. Pour into an ice cream freezer container. Freeze using the manufacturer's directions.

Sally Bickerstaff Hatcher

Peach Ice Cream

Serves 8

1 quart small peaches, peeled and mashed (about 10 small)
2 cups sugar
1 quart half-and-half
3 drops of almond extract

Mix the peaches with 1 cup of the sugar in a bowl. Chill in the refrigerator. Combine the remaining 1 cup sugar and the half-and-half in a bowl and mix well. Chill in the refrigerator.

Place the half-and-half mixture in an ice cream freezer container. Stir in the almond extract. Freeze using the manufacturer's directions until semi-firm. Add the peach mixture. Continue freezing until firm.

Oscar Leon Betts, Jr.

"The Recipe"

Serves 6 to 8

This recipe is from Alice Gentry Douglas, who serves it in silver goblets when she hosts family and friends at Sunday night supper.

1 gallon vanilla ice cream
1 1/4 to 1 1/2 cups coffee-flavored or espresso-flavored vodka

Let the ice cream stand at room temperature for 10 minutes to soften. Process one-half of the ice cream and one-half of the vodka in a blender until smooth. Repeat with the remaining ice cream and vodka. Place in the freezer until ready to serve.

Ginny Hendrix Lawrence

Chocolate Syrup

Serves 8

1 cup (6 ounces) chocolate chips
1 (14-ounce) can sweetened condensed milk
1/3 cup milk
1/4 cup brandy

Melt the chocolate chips in a saucepan. Stir in the condensed milk. Add the milk and mix well. Stir in the brandy. Pour into a medium bowl. Chill in the refrigerator.

Michelle Moorman Caves

Strawberries and Cream

Serves 3 or 4

Serve this simple, light, delicious dessert with a glass of Champagne for a special occasion.

12 to 16 fresh whole strawberries
1 cup sour cream
1 cup packed brown sugar

Dip each whole strawberry in the sour cream. Roll in the brown sugar.

Cortney Lynch Douglas

Cream Cheese Pound Cake

Serves 12 to 14

1 1/2 cups (3 sticks) butter, softened
8 ounces cream cheese, softened
3 cups sugar
Dash of salt
1 1/2 teaspoons vanilla extract
6 eggs
3 cups sifted cake flour

Cream the butter, cream cheese and sugar in a mixing bowl until light and fluffy. Add the salt and vanilla and mix well. Add the eggs one at a time, beating well after each addition. Stir in the flour. Spoon into a greased and floured tube pan or bundt pan. Bake at 325 degrees for 1 1/2 hours or until the cake tests done. Cool in the pan for 10 minutes. Invert onto a serving plate.

Martha Gilliam Hatcher

Sour Cream Pound Cake

Serves 12

As a young girl, I would pull up my great-grandmother's hand-carved kitchen chair to the counter to help her add the ingredients for this cake as she stirred them by hand with a wooden spoon. She swore that stirring by hand with the wooden spoon was the secret to this recipe.

3 tablespoons all-purpose flour	3 cups all-purpose flour
1 cup (2 sticks) butter, softened	1/4 teaspoon baking soda
3 cups sugar	1 cup sour cream
5 eggs	2 teaspoons butter flavoring

Grease a bundt pan and sprinkle with 3 tablespoons flour. Cream the butter and sugar in a mixing bowl. Add the eggs one at a time, beating well after each addition. Add 3 cups flour and the baking soda and mix well. Stir in the sour cream and butter flavoring. Spoon into the prepared pan. Bake at 325 degrees for 1 hour. Reduce the oven temperature to 300 degrees. Bake for 30 to 40 minutes longer or until the cake tests done. Cool in the pan for 10 minutes. Invert onto a serving plate.

Stacey Lamberth Boyd

Whipping Cream Pound Cake

Serves 10 to 12

In the South, we like our pound cake served with fresh berries or ice cream or toasted in the oven for a delicious morning treat with coffee.

1 1/2 cups (3 sticks) butter, softened	3 1/2 cups cake flour, sifted
3 cups (heaping) sugar	1 cup whipping cream
6 eggs	1 teaspoon almond extract

Cream the butter and sugar in a mixing bowl until light and fluffy. Add the eggs one at a time, beating well after each addition. Add the flour and cream alternately, beating constantly. Stir in the almond extract. Spoon into a greased 10-inch bundt pan. Bake at 300 degrees for 1 1/2 hours. Cool in the pan for 10 minutes. Invert onto a serving plate.

Lauren Brazil Briscoe

Miss Nancy's Carrot Cake

Serves 8 to 10

Cake
2 cups all-purpose flour
2 teaspoons salt
2 teaspoons baking soda
2 teaspoons (heaping) cinnamon
2 cups sugar
3/4 cup vegetable oil
4 eggs
3/4 cup buttermilk
3 cups grated carrots

Nutty Cream Cheese Frosting
8 ounces cream cheese, softened
1/2 cup (1 stick) margarine, softened
1 cup confectioners' sugar
1 cup pecans, chopped

To prepare the cake, mix the flour, salt, baking soda and cinnamon together. Beat the sugar and oil in the bowl of an electric mixer fitted with a paddle attachment. Add the eggs one at a time, beating well after each addition. Add the flour mixture and buttermilk alternately, beating constantly. Stir in the carrots. Spoon evenly into three greased and floured 9-inch cake pans. Bake at 350 degrees for 20 minutes. Cool in the pans for 10 minutes. Invert onto a wire rack to cool completely.

To prepare the frosting, beat the cream cheese and margarine in a mixing bowl until smooth and creamy. Add the confectioners' sugar and beat until smooth. Stir in the pecans. Spread between the layers and over the top and side of the cake.

Dori Sponcler Jones

"*E*dge of my seat" means something is exciting and suspenseful.

Peppermint Christmas Cake

Serves 12

Cake
2 cups all-purpose flour
1 1/4 teaspoons baking soda
1/4 teaspoon baking powder
1 teaspoon salt
2/3 cup butter, softened
1 2/3 cups sugar
3 eggs
1/2 teaspoon vanilla extract
1 1/3 cups water

Peppermint Frosting
8 ounces cream cheese, softened
1 cup (2 sticks) butter, softened
2 (1-pound) packages confectioners' sugar
2 teaspoons peppermint extract
15 round peppermint candies, crushed

To prepare the cake, mix the flour, baking soda, baking powder and salt together. Beat the butter, sugar, eggs and vanilla at high speed in a mixing bowl for 3 minutes. Add the flour mixture alternately with the water, beating constantly. Spoon into two greased and floured 9-inch cake pans. Bake at 350 degrees for 30 to 35 minutes or until a wooden pick inserted into the center comes out clean. Cool in the cake pans for 10 minutes. Invert onto a wire rack to cool completely.

To prepare the frosting, beat the cream cheese and butter in a mixing bowl until smooth. Add the confectioners' sugar gradually, beating constantly until smooth. Stir in the peppermint extract. Spread between the layers and over the top and side of the cake. Sprinkle the top with the crushed candies.

Charlotte Lee Bowman

Every Christmas Eve, the children gathered in the living room for my grandfather, Jess, to read 'Twas the Night Before Christmas. He always sat on our big sofa in the living room with all the grandchildren piled around him. Although we've lost Jess, I knew he was with us in spirit when I saw my two-year-old son and niece curled up next to my husband in the living room as he read the same story with his own style, creating a new tradition.

— Mary Lynn Pugh Grubb

Red Velvet Cake

Serves 12 to 14

*Nothing is more beautiful than Red Velvet Cake for Christmas.
Make this cake for the holidays, and Santa is certain to be good to you!*

Cake
2 1/2 cups all-purpose flour
1 teaspoon salt
1 teaspoon baking soda
2 teaspoons baking cocoa
1 cup buttermilk
1 teaspoon vinegar
1 teaspoon vanilla extract
2 cups vegetable oil
1 1/2 cups sugar
2 eggs
1 ounce red food coloring

Cream Cheese Frosting
3/4 cup (1 1/2 sticks) margarine, softened
12 ounces cream cheese, softened
1 1/2 (1-pound) packages
confectioners' sugar
1 1/2 teaspoons vanilla extract
1 1/2 cups chopped pecans, or
3/4 cup chopped pecans and
3/4 cup chopped walnuts

To prepare the cake, sift the flour, salt, baking soda and baking cocoa together. Mix the buttermilk, vinegar and vanilla in a small bowl. Beat the oil and sugar in a mixing bowl. Add the eggs one at a time, beating well after each addition. Stir in the food coloring carefully. Add the buttermilk mixture and the flour mixture alternately, beating constantly. Pour into four well-greased 8-inch cake pans. Bake at 350 degrees for 35 to 40 minutes or until the layers test done, checking the layers after 25 minutes. Cool in the pans for 10 minutes. Invert onto a wire rack to cool completely.

To prepare the frosting, cream the margarine and cream cheese in a mixing bowl. Add the confectioners' sugar and vanilla and beat until smooth. Stir in the pecans.

To assemble, brush the crumbs off the cake layers. Spread the frosting between the layers and over the top and side of the cake.

Note: For a level cake, lay the first two layers face down on a
cake plate and the last two layers face up.

Barbara Brettel Peacock

Callaway Rum Cake

Serves 16

*Beth Callaway's Rum Cake has been a Columbus favorite since
she began baking them in 1985. Beth would make up to ninety rum cakes
every Christmas to give as gifts. Recipients always love to see
a member of the Callaway family coming with cake in hand stating,
"We've come bearing rum cake!"*

1 (2-layer) package golden butter-recipe cake mix
1 (4-ounce) package vanilla instant pudding mix
4 eggs
1/2 cup rum
1/2 cup water
1/2 cup vegetable oil
1 cup sugar
1/2 cup (1 stick) butter
1/4 cup rum
1/4 cup water

Beat the cake mix, pudding mix, eggs, 1/2 cup rum, 1/2 cup water and the oil in a mixing bowl for 3 minutes. Pour into a well-greased and floured bundt pan. Bake at 350 degrees for 1 hour.

Bring the sugar, butter, 1/4 cup rum and 1/4 cup water to a boil in a saucepan over medium heat. Boil for 3 minutes, stirring frequently. Remove the cake from the oven. Pour the sauce over the cake immediately. Let stand until the sauce is absorbed. Invert the warm cake onto a serving plate.

Jennings Adams DeWitt Palmer

Old-Fashioned Apple Pie

Serves 8

2 unbaked (10-inch) frozen deep-dish pie shells	1/2 cup golden raisins
	1/2 teaspoon cinnamon
6 Granny Smith apples, peeled	2 tablespoons lemon juice
1/2 cup (1 stick) butter or margarine	2 tablespoons cornstarch
3/4 cup sugar	1 egg, beaten

Thaw one of the pie shells. Cut the apples into thin slices or wedges. Melt the butter in a large saucepan over medium heat. Add the apples. Cook for 4 to 5 minutes. Stir in the sugar. Add the raisins and cinnamon and mix well. Mix the lemon juice and cornstarch in a bowl. Stir into the apple mixture. Remove from the heat. Pour into the thawed pie shell. Place the frozen pie shell upside down on top and let stand for 15 minutes before removing the pan. Remove the pan from the top pie shell carefully. Crimp the edges of both pie shells together with a fork. Brush the egg over the top pie shell. Cut several vents in the top. Bake at 375 degrees for 20 minutes. Rotate the pie in the oven 180 degrees. Bake for 20 minutes longer.

Lisa Thigpen Beyer

Blueberry Pie

Serves 6 to 8

4 cups blueberries	5 or 6 pats of butter
1/2 cup packed light brown sugar	1 egg
1/2 cup granulated sugar	Milk for brushing
1 teaspoon fresh lemon juice	2 to 3 tablespoons granulated sugar
2 unbaked (10-inch) deep-dish pie shells	Vanilla ice cream

Mix the blueberries, brown sugar, granulated sugar and lemon juice in a bowl. Spoon into one of the pie shells and top with the butter. Roll the remaining pie shell on a lightly floured surface with a floured rolling pin. Cut the desired pattern into the pastry. Place over the top of the pie, sealing and crimping the edge. Mix the egg with a small amount of milk in a bowl. Brush over the pastry. Sprinkle with 2 to 3 tablespoons granulated sugar. Bake at 400 degrees for 45 to 50 minutes or until golden brown. Remove from the oven and cool for 15 minutes. Serve with ice cream. For a firmer filling, mix a little cornstarch with the sugar. If you use frozen blueberries, thaw and drain.

Ernest Smallman IV

Buttermilk Pie

Makes 2 pies

In the South, we are known for extravagant spreads of food brought when there is a death in the family. On one such occasion, Alice Metcalf, a neighbor and past Junior League member, brought the most divine buttermilk pie. My husband loved it so much that she went home and immediately baked two more pies and passed them, along with the recipe, over the back fence.

2 unbaked (9-inch) pie shells
3 tablespoons all-purpose flour
3 cups sugar
6 eggs, beaten
3/4 cup (1 1/2 sticks) butter, melted

1 cup buttermilk
1 tablespoon lemon juice
1 teaspoon vanilla extract
Nutmeg for sprinkling

Prepare the pie shells using the package directions. Mix the flour and sugar in a large mixing bowl. Add the eggs and mix well. Stir in the butter and buttermilk. Add the lemon juice and vanilla and mix well. Spoon into the pie shells and sprinkle with nutmeg. Bake at 425 degrees for 10 minutes. Reduce the oven temperature to 350 degrees. Bake for 35 minutes longer or until golden brown. Serve with whipped topping or whipped cream on the side.

Millie Peacock Patrick

"*Chip and a chair*" *is a poker term: as long as you have a chip and a chair, you're still alive.*

Peanut Butter Pie

Serves 8 to 10

1¹/4 cups (7¹/2 ounces) semisweet chocolate chips
1¹/2 cups heavy whipping cream
2 tablespoons butter
1 (9-inch) graham cracker pie shell

1/2 cup heavy whipping cream
8 ounces cream cheese, softened
1 cup creamy peanut butter
1 cup sugar
2 peanut butter granola bars, crushed

Combine the chocolate chips, 1¹/2 cups cream and the butter in a saucepan. Heat over low heat until the chocolate and butter are melted, stirring constantly. Pour into the pie shell and coat evenly, reserving a small amount of the chocolate mixture. Let stand until set.

Beat 1/2 cup cream in a mixing bowl until soft peaks form. Beat the cream cheese and peanut butter in a mixing bowl until smooth. Add the sugar and mix well. Fold in the whipped cream. Spoon into the prepared pie shell. Chill for 4 hours or longer. Sprinkle with the crushed granola bars. Melt the reserved chocolate mixture and drizzle over the top.

Michelle Williams Hudson

Light Toffee Bit Pie

Serves 8

3 ounces light cream cheese, softened
2 tablespoons sugar
1/2 cup half-and-half
8 ounces fat-free whipped topping

1 (8-ounce) package milk chocolate English toffee bits
1 (9-inch) reduced-fat graham cracker pie shell

Beat the cream cheese and sugar in a mixing bowl until smooth. Add the half-and-half and beat until blended. Fold in the whipped topping and 1 cup of the toffee bits. Spoon into the pie shell. Sprinkle with the remaining toffee bits. Freeze, covered, for 8 to 10 hours. Remove from the freezer and let stand for 10 minutes before serving.

Wendy Ryan Gay

Caramel Brownies

Serves 24

1 (14-ounce) package caramels
1 (5-ounce) can evaporated milk
1 (2-layer) package German chocolate cake mix

3/4 cup (11/2 sticks) butter, softened
1 cup (6 ounces) milk chocolate chips

Place the caramels and one-half of the evaporated milk in a microwave-safe bowl. Microwave on High for 2 minutes, stirring halfway through. Microwave for 2 minutes longer or until the caramels are melted, stirring at 30-second intervals.

Combine the cake mix, butter and remaining evaporated milk in a bowl and mix well. Pat one-half of the mixture into a 9×13-inch baking dish. Bake at 350 degrees for 8 minutes. Remove from the oven and maintain the oven temperature. Sprinkle with the chocolate chips. Spread the caramel mixture over the chocolate chips. Pat the remaining cake mix mixture into patties and arrange over the top, leaving lots of space between them. Bake for 30 minutes or until the brownies pull from the sides of the pan. Cut into squares. Remove from the oven and cool completely before serving.

Shriver Jones Tommey

Chocolate Chip Oatmeal Cookies

Makes 3 to 4 dozen

21/2 cups all-purpose flour
1/2 teaspoon baking soda
1/4 teaspoon salt
1 cup (2 sticks) butter, softened
1 cup packed brown sugar
1/2 cup granulated sugar

2 eggs
2 teaspoons vanilla extract
2 cups (12 ounces) semisweet chocolate chips
2 cups rolled oats

Mix the flour, baking soda and salt together. Beat the butter, brown sugar and granulated sugar at low speed in a mixing bowl until smooth. Add the eggs one at a time, beating well after each addition. Add the vanilla 1 teaspoon at a time. Do not overmix. Add the flour mixture gradually. Stir in the chocolate chips and oats. Drop by spoonfuls onto greased cookie sheets. Bake at 300 degrees for 12 to 15 minutes or until brown. Cool on wire racks.

Dori Sponcler Jones

Oatmeal Lace Cookies

Makes 2 dozen

1/2 cup all-purpose flour	2 tablespoons light corn syrup
1/4 teaspoon baking powder	2 tablespoons heavy cream
1/2 cup sugar	1/3 cup margarine, softened
1/2 cup quick-cooking oats	1 teaspoon vanilla extract

Stir the flour, baking powder and sugar in a mixing bowl. Add the oats, corn syrup, cream, margarine and vanilla and beat until blended. Drop by teaspoonfuls onto a foil-lined cookie sheet. Bake at 375 degrees for 6 to 8 minutes or until light brown. Let stand for 1 minute. Remove from the cookie sheet.

Leita Trammell Coleman

Cashew Drop Cookies

Makes 90 to 100

Cookies	Brown Butter Frosting
4 cups all-purpose flour	1 cup (2 sticks) butter
1 1/2 teaspoons baking soda	4 cups confectioners' sugar
1 1/2 teaspoons baking powder	6 tablespoons heavy whipping cream
1 cup (2 sticks) butter, softened	1/2 teaspoon vanilla extract
2 cups packed brown sugar	Whole cashews for garnish
2 eggs	
1 teaspoon vanilla extract	
2/3 cup sour cream	
3 cups salted cashews, chopped	

To prepare the cookies, mix the flour, baking soda and baking powder together. Beat the butter and brown sugar in a mixing bowl until light and fluffy. Add the eggs and vanilla and mix well. Beat in the sour cream at low speed. Add the flour mixture and beat well. Stir in the cashews. Drop by rounded spoonfuls onto two greased large cookie sheets. Bake at 350 degrees for 12 minutes or until light brown. Remove to wire racks to cool. Repeat with the remaining dough.

To prepare the frosting, melt the butter in a saucepan over medium heat until light brown. Remove from the heat. Whisk in the confectioners' sugar, cream and vanilla until smooth. Spread over the cookies. Garnish each with a whole cashew.

Margaret Marston Ward

Peanut Butter Blossoms

Makes 12 to 15

3 egg whites
1 cup sugar
1 cup crunchy peanut butter
Pinch of salt

Beat the egg whites in a mixing bowl until stiff peaks form. Fold in the sugar, peanut butter and salt. Drop by teaspoonfuls onto a greased cookie sheet. Bake at 325 degrees for 12 minutes. Cool on a wire rack.

Elaine Tribble McMillen

Pecan Praline Strips

Serves 8 to 10

24 graham cracker squares
1 cup packed light brown sugar
1/2 cup (1 stick) margarine
1/2 cup (1 stick) butter
1 cup chopped pecans

Arrange the graham crackers in a foil-lined 10×15-inch baking pan. Bring the brown sugar, margarine and butter to a slow rolling boil in a saucepan. Boil for 3 to 4 minutes. Stir in the pecans. Spread over the graham crackers. Bake at 350 degrees for 10 to 12 minutes. Remove from the oven. Cut into strips while still warm. Let stand until cool. Remove from the pan.

Donna Sears Hand

Sugar Cookies

Makes 4 dozen

Sprinkle with green sprinkles for the perfect St. Patrick's Day treat, or make the Fourth of July pop with colorful red, white, and blue sugar crystals.

3 cups all-purpose flour	2 eggs
3/4 teaspoon baking powder	1/4 cup light corn syrup
1/2 teaspoon baking soda	1 tablespoon vanilla extract
1/2 teaspoon salt	4 tablespoons all-purpose flour
1 1/4 cups granulated sugar	Granulated sugar or colored sugar crystals
1 cup shortening	for sprinkling (optional)

Mix 3 cups flour, the baking powder, baking soda and salt together. Beat 1 1/4 cups sugar and the shortening at medium speed in a large mixing bowl until blended. Add the eggs, corn syrup and vanilla and beat until fluffy. Add the flour mixture gradually, beating constantly at low speed.

Divide the dough into four equal portions. Spread 1 tablespoon flour on a large sheet of waxed paper. Place one portion of the dough on the prepared waxed paper. Cover with another large sheet of waxed paper. Roll the dough 1/4 inch thick. Cut with a floured cookie cutter. Place 2 inches apart on an ungreased cookie sheet. Sprinkle with granulated sugar. Repeat with the remaining flour and dough portions. Bake at 375 degrees for 5 to 9 minutes or until light brown. Remove to a wire rack to cool.

Note: If the dough is too sticky or too soft to roll, wrap each portion with plastic wrap and chill for 1 hour or longer.

Jennifer Hartley Glover

"You can't deny laughter; when it comes, it plops down in your favorite chair and stays as long as it wants."

—*Stephen King*

Baboo's Scotcheroos

Serves 6

1 cup sugar	6 cups crisp rice cereal
1 cup light corn syrup	6 ounces chocolate bits
1 cup peanut butter	6 ounces caramel bits

Melt the sugar with the corn syrup in a 3-quart saucepan, stirring frequently. Bring to a boil and remove from the heat. Add the peanut butter and stir until smooth. Add the cereal and mix well. Press into a well-buttered 9×13-inch glass dish with a plastic bag over your hand. Melt the chocolate bits and caramel bits in a saucepan, stirring constantly. Spread over the cereal mixture. Let stand until cool. Cut into squares.

Susan Davis Bock

White Chocolate Chip Macadamia Nut Cookies

Makes 30

1 cup plus 2 tablespoons all-purpose flour	1/2 cup (1 stick) unsalted butter, softened
1/2 teaspoon baking soda	1/2 cup packed light brown sugar
1/2 teaspoon kosher salt	1/2 cup granulated sugar
1 egg	1 cup (6 ounces) white chocolate chips
1 teaspoon vanilla extract	3/4 cup macadamia nuts, chopped

Mix the flour, baking soda and kosher salt together. Beat the egg and vanilla in a small bowl. Place the butter, brown sugar and granulated sugar in the bowl of a stand mixer fitted with the paddle attachment. Beat at medium speed for 20 seconds or just until mixed. Scrape down the side of the bowl. Add the egg mixture and beat well. Add the flour mixture gradually, beating at low speed just until mixed. Stir in the white chocolate chips and macadamia nuts. Drop by rounded tablespoonfuls 2 inches apart onto cookie sheets sprayed with nonstick cooking spray. Bake at 375 degrees for 10 to 12 minutes or until golden brown. Cool on a wire rack.

Claudia Sessions Garrard

Front Porch Buckeyes

Makes 4 dozen

1 cup (2 sticks) butter or margarine, softened
1 (1-pound) package confectioners' sugar

1 cup creamy peanut butter
10 ounces semisweet chocolate chips
1/2 block paraffin

Combine the butter, confectioners' sugar and peanut butter in a bowl and mix well. Shape into 1-inch balls and place on waxed paper-lined baking sheets. Chill for 1 hour or until firm.

Melt the chocolate chips and paraffin in a double boiler over hot water. Dip the balls into the chocolate mixture using wooden picks, leaving the top section uncovered to create the "buckeye" effect. Return to the baking sheets. Chill until set. Store in an airtight container with waxed paper between each layer in the refrigerator for several days.

Colleen Day Rustin

Front Porch Buckeyes bring back many memories of my grandmother and special times spent with her. She always had them in the refrigerator whenever I spent time at my grandparents' house in the summer. We would go for walks down to the "square" in their small Southern town in Georgia. When we would return home, we were always hot, and we would sit on the wooden swing on her screened-in porch and read books while we drank lemonade and ate buckeyes.

— Colleen Day Rustin

From High Chairs to Highbacks

Children's Cuisine
& Confections

When my mother, Margaret Flournoy, was a child in 1921, she walked with her mother

from 802 Broad Street to the Josephs' house at 828 Broad Street (now Broadway).

While visiting, she became very attached to this "child's" chair. After many tears were shed

when she didn't want to leave the chair, the Josephs graciously gave it to her to take home as her own.

In the years to come, her children and grandchildren enjoyed sitting in this little chair in the kitchen

watching as meals were prepared. Like many Columbus families, we enjoy the benefits of

raising children surrounded by friends and family where even a treasured small chair

can tie several generations together.

—Mary Bickerstaff Bradley

From High Chairs to Highbacks

Children's Cuisine & Confections

Cheesy Cheese Dots

Makes 1 dozen

2 cups (8 ounces) shredded mozzarella cheese
2 cups (8 ounces) shredded sharp Cheddar cheese
Dash of garlic salt

Spray twelve muffin cups lightly with nonstick cooking spray. Sprinkle a thin layer of the mozzarella cheese and then a thin layer of the Cheddar cheese in each prepared muffin cup. Sprinkle with garlic salt. Bake at 350 degrees for 5 minutes or until set and golden brown around the edges. Remove to paper towels to cool slightly. Serve warm.

Margaret Glenn Church and Rachel Anne Grier

Fun Mix

Serves 10 to 12

1 (8-ounce) package traditional Chex Mix
1 cup raisins
1 1/2 cups Cheddar goldfish crackers
1 cup salted peanuts
1 cup honey sesame sticks

Combine the Chex Mix, raisins, goldfish crackers, peanuts and sesame sticks in a large sealable plastic bag. Seal the bag and shake to mix.

Dori Sponcler Jones

Pigs in a Blanket

Makes 32

1 (16-ounce) package smoked beef
cocktail sausages
1 (8-count) can refrigerator crescent rolls

Brown the sausages in a skillet over medium heat for 8 to 10 minutes; drain on paper towels. Unroll the crescent roll dough and separate into triangles. Cut four small triangles out of each large triangle. Place one sausage on each small triangle and roll from the wide ends to enclose. Arrange on a baking sheet. Bake at 375 degrees for 8 to 10 minutes or until golden brown.

Shannan Hartley Bickerstaff

Ants on a Log

Serves 1

1 banana
2 teaspoons peanut butter
Raisins to taste

Cut the banana crosswise into halves. Cut each half lengthwise into halves. Spread the peanut butter on the cut side of each half and dot with raisins to resemble ants.

Olivia Cheves Blanchard

"Sushi" Rolls

Serves 2

The carrot and cucumber matchstick pieces can be created using a julienne peeler or mandoline slicer. For quick preparation, many supermarkets sell vegetables already pre-cut into matchstick pieces.

2 slices whole wheat sandwich bread
3 tablespoons reduced-fat cream cheese
1¹/2 tablespoons reduced-fat sour cream
4 carrot matchsticks
4 cucumber matchsticks

Flatten the bread slices with a rolling pin. Mix the cream cheese and sour cream in a bowl until smooth. Spread the cream cheese mixture evenly over the bread slices. Lay 2 carrot sticks and 2 cucumber sticks at the bottom of each bread slice with the ends hanging over the edge. Roll up and press the ends gently to seal. Cut each roll-up into four equal portions.

Hadley Upchurch Scott

Piñata Soup

Serves 12

2 pounds ground beef
2 envelopes taco seasoning mix
2 envelopes ranch salad dressing mix
2 (16-ounce) cans whole kernel white corn
1 (16-ounce) can black beans
1 (16-ounce) can pinto beans
1 (16-ounce) can kidney beans
1 (10-ounce) can tomatoes with green chiles
1 (16-ounce) can diced tomatoes
1 to 2 cups water
Sour cream for garnish
Shredded Cheddar cheese for garnish
Sliced green onions for garnish

Brown the ground beef in a large deep skillet, stirring until crumbly; drain. Add the taco seasoning mix, salad dressing mix, undrained vegetables and water and mix well. Simmer for 2 hours. Ladle into soup bowls. Garnish with sour cream, Cheddar cheese and green onions. Serve with tortillas or corn bread.

Beth Lewis Williams

Egg in the Hole

Serves 1

Kids love this easy breakfast treat, and it goes well with grits.

2 slices white bread or wheat bread   2 eggs
1 tablespoon butter or butter substitute   Salt and pepper to taste

Make a hole in the center of each bread slice with a biscuit cutter or small glass. Melt the butter in a skillet over medium-high heat. Add the bread. Cook until light brown. Turn the bread. Break one egg into each hole. Cook for 2 minutes or until the eggs are set, turning again if needed for desired firmness. Sprinkle with salt and pepper. Serve warm.

Edie Pendleton Evans

Grand Slam Granola Bars

Serves 12

You can add other ingredients such as chocolate chips, peanut butter, or cranberries.

4 cups rolled oats   1 egg
1 cup (2 sticks) butter or   1/2 teaspoon vanilla extract
margarine, melted   1 cup chopped pecans
2/3 cup packed brown sugar   1 cup raisins
1/2 cup honey

Spread the oats in an ungreased 10×15-inch baking pan. Bake at 350 degrees for 15 minutes, stirring every 5 minutes. Remove from the oven. Maintain the oven temperature.

Combine the butter, brown sugar, honey, egg, vanilla, pecans and raisins in a large bowl and mix well. Add the oats and mix well. Spread evenly in a lightly greased 10×15-inch baking pan. Bake for 25 minutes. Remove from the oven and let stand to cool completely. Cut into bars.

Mia Knighton Rice

Glorified Grilled Cheese

Serves 4

4 slices mozzarella cheese	4 dashes of dried basil
8 slices white wheat bread	2 tablespoons margarine
1 tomato, sliced	

Place a slice of cheese on one-half of the bread slices. Lay 1 or 2 slices of tomato over the cheese. Sprinkle each with a dash of basil. Top with the remaining bread slices. Melt the margarine in a skillet. Add the sandwiches. Cook until brown on each side, turning once and holding together if the cheese doesn't stick to both sides.

Leslie Marie Holloway

Cheeseburger, Cheeseburger

Serves 5

1 pound ground beef	10 frozen yeast dinner rolls, thawed
1 tablespoon Worcestershire sauce	10 teaspoons ketchup (optional)
1 teaspoon onion powder	10 teaspoons mustard (optional)
1 teaspoon garlic salt	5 slices American cheese, cut into halves
1 teaspoon pepper	2 tablespoons butter, melted
1 teaspoon dried parsley	

Mix the ground beef, Worcestershire sauce, onion powder, garlic salt, pepper and parsley in a bowl using your hands. Shape into ten patties 2 1/2 inches in diameter. Heat a cast-iron skillet or grill pan over medium-high heat. Lightly spray the hot skillet with nonstick cooking spray. Cook the patties in batches in the prepared skillet for 7 minutes or until cooked through, turning once.

Cut the dinner rolls into halves horizontally. Place 1 teaspoon of the ketchup on the cut side of the top half of each roll. Place 1 teaspoon of the mustard on the cut side of the bottom half of each roll. Place a cooked patty on the bottom half of each roll and top with one piece of the cheese. Replace the top halves of the rolls and place the cheeseburgers on a baking sheet. Brush the tops with the butter. Bake at 350 degrees for 12 minutes or until the tops are light brown and the cheese melts. Serve with condiments of choice.

Mary Lynn Pugh Grubb

Ham and Cheese Super Heroes

Serves 10

2 (20-count) packages party rolls
3 tablespoons mustard
3 tablespoons mayonnaise

8 ounces ham, thinly sliced
6 ounces American cheese, thinly sliced
1/4 cup (1/2 stick) butter, melted

Partially freeze the rolls. Remove the rolls intact from the foil pans and cut into halves horizontally. Mix the mustard and mayonnaise in a small bowl. Spread over the cut side of the bottom half of the rolls and return to the pans. Layer the ham and cheese over the mustard mixture. Replace the top halves and brush with butter. Bake, wrapped in foil, at 400 degrees for 10 minutes. Cut into slices and serve.

Katy Pugh Cone

Cheesy Chicken Croissants

Serves 8

Children love this recipe and really enjoy getting their hands dirty mixing the chicken and cheese.

2 boneless skinless chicken breasts
1 (10-ounce) can cream of chicken soup
1 (10-ounce) can cream of mushroom soup
1 cup (4 ounces) shredded sharp Cheddar cheese

1 cup (4 ounces) shredded Monterey Jack cheese
1 (8-count) can refrigerator crescent rolls
1/2 cup (2 ounces) shredded sharp Cheddar cheese
1/2 cup (2 ounces) shredded Monterey Jack cheese

Cook the chicken in boiling water in a saucepan for 30 minutes or until cooked through. Drain and let stand until cool. Heat the chicken soup and mushroom soup in a saucepan until heated through, stirring constantly. Shred the chicken into a large bowl. Add 1 cup Cheddar cheese and 1 cup Monterey Jack cheese and mix well. Unroll the crescent roll dough and separate into triangles. Place a tightly packed scoop of the chicken mixture in the center of each triangle. Bring up the corners of each triangle to enclose the filling to form "pocketbooks" and press to seal. Arrange in a 9×13-inch baking dish so the sides do not touch. Pour the soup mixture over the top and around the sides. Sprinkle with 1/2 cup Cheddar cheese and 1/2 cup Monterey Jack cheese. Bake at 350 degrees for 25 to 35 minutes or until puffy and light brown.

Mara Hall Kelly

Chicken Potpie

Serves 6 to 8

This recipe is also delicious with the addition of cooked carrots, peas, or green beans.

1 small chicken	1 teaspoon salt
2 chicken breasts	Pepper to taste
Salt to taste	3 cups (or more) chicken broth
2 refrigerator pie pastries	1/4 cup (1/2 stick) butter
1 cup chopped celery	1/2 cup all-purpose flour
1 cup chopped onion	2 cups half-and-half

Simmer the chicken in salted water in a saucepan until tender. Remove from the heat to cool. Drain the chicken. Tear the chicken into bite-size pieces, discarding the skin and bones. Press one pie pastry into a lightly greased 2-quart baking dish and prick the bottom. Bake at 400 degrees for 4 minutes. Remove from the oven. Reduce the oven temperature to 350 degrees.

Cook the celery and onion with 1 teaspoon salt and pepper in 2 cups of the broth in a saucepan for 7 minutes; drain. Melt the butter in a medium saucepan. Stir in the flour until smooth. Cook over medium heat for 2 to 3 minutes. Add the remaining 1 cup broth gradually. Cook until thickened, stirring constantly. Add salt and pepper to taste. Stir in the half-and-half a small amount at a time. Cook until thickened, stirring constantly. Remove from the heat. Add the vegetables. Add additional broth if the sauce is too thick.

Layer the chicken in the prebaked piecrust. Pour the vegetable mixture over the chicken. Top with the remaining pie pastry; cut several vents in the pastry. Bake for 30 to 45 minutes or until the pastry is golden brown.

Laura Schomburg Patrick

When I was in the fourth grade, I accidentally pulled a chair out from under my dad at church. We were on the front row and I moved his chair closer to mine. He ended up sitting on the floor! The congregation broke up laughing.

— Charlotte Lee Bowman

Pizzazzy Pizza

Serves 10

1 garlic clove, minced	2 whole wheat thin pizza crusts
1 teaspoon olive oil	1 (15-ounce) can pizza sauce
2 cups chopped mixed onions, tomatoes and green bell peppers	2 cups (8 ounces) shredded Cheddar cheese
3 tablespoons chopped basil	2 cups (8 ounces) shredded Italian 6-cheese blend
Salt and pepper to taste	

Sauté the garlic in the olive oil in a skillet over medium heat for 1 minute. Add the vegetable mixture. Sauté for 7 minutes or until soft. Add the basil, salt and pepper. Top each pizza crust with the pizza sauce, Cheddar cheese, Italian cheese blend and the sautéed vegetable mixture. Place directly on the oven rack. Bake at 450 degrees for 8 to 10 minutes or until the cheese melts.

Mary Lynn Pugh Grubb

Chicken and Broccoli Casserole

Serves 4 to 6

2 stalks broccoli spears	1/4 to 1/2 teaspoon curry powder
4 chicken breasts, cooked and cut into bite-size pieces	1 cup (4 ounces) shredded sharp Cheddar cheese
1 (10-ounce) can cream of chicken soup	Bread crumbs or crushed crackers for sprinkling
1/2 cup mayonnaise	
1 1/2 to 2 tablespoons lemon juice	

Steam the broccoli until barely tender; drain. Cut the broccoli into small pieces. Place the broccoli in individual small ramekins and cover with the chicken. Mix the soup, mayonnaise, lemon juice and curry powder in a bowl. Pour over the chicken. Sprinkle with the cheese and bread crumbs. Bake at 350 degrees for 20 minutes.

Gardiner Zollo Church

Crunchy Baked Drumsticks

Serves 6

4 eggs, lightly beaten
1/2 teaspoon salt
1/2 teaspoon black pepper
4 cups crushed cornflakes
1 cup (4 ounces) grated Parmesan cheese

1/2 teaspoon cayenne pepper
1/2 teaspoon garlic salt
12 chicken drumsticks
1/4 cup (1/2 stick) butter, melted

Position an oven rack in the upper third of the oven. Line a baking sheet with foil and spray with nonstick cooking spray. Mix the eggs, salt and black pepper in a medium bowl. Mix the cornflakes, cheese, cayenne pepper and garlic salt in a large bowl. Dip each drumstick in the egg mixture and coat with the cornflake mixture. Place on the prepared baking sheet, pressing the remaining cornflake mixture on the top of each drumstick. Drizzle with the butter. Bake at 450 degrees for 30 minutes or until brown and cooked through.

Lisa Spafford Brown

Baked Chicken with Honey Dip

Serves 4

Honey Dip

1 cup light sour cream
2 teaspoons honey
1 teaspoon Dijon mustard
1 teaspoon salt

Chicken

1 tablespoon extra-virgin olive oil
3 boneless skinless chicken breasts
1 cup milk

1 teaspoon salt
1 teaspoon black pepper
1 1/4 cups (5 ounces) grated
  Parmesan cheese
1 cup whole wheat panko
  (Japanese bread crumbs)
1 tablespoon Italian seasoning
1/4 teaspoon cayenne pepper
2 tablespoons extra-virgin olive oil

To prepare the dip, combine the sour cream, honey, Dijon mustard and salt in a bowl and mix well. Chill until serving time.

To prepare the chicken, line a heavy baking sheet with foil and brush with 1 tablespoon olive oil. Cut each chicken breast into 3 or 4 strips. Place the chicken and milk in a bowl and stir to coat. Stir in the salt and black pepper. Let stand for 15 minutes. Mix the cheese, panko, Italian seasoning and cayenne pepper in a bowl. Drain the chicken. Coat the chicken with the panko mixture, pressing to adhere. Arrange evenly spaced in a single layer on the prepared baking sheet. Sprinkle with any remaining panko mixture. Drizzle with 2 tablespoons olive oil. Bake at 500 degrees for 12 minutes or until cooked through and golden brown. Serve with the dip.

Katy Pugh Cone

Poppy Seed Chicken

Serves 4 to 6

2 cups chopped cooked chicken
1 cup sour cream
1 (10-ounce) can cream of chicken soup

40 butter crackers, crushed
1/2 cup (1 stick) butter, melted
2 teaspoons poppy seeds

Layer the chicken in an 8×8-inch baking dish. Mix the sour cream and soup in a bowl until smooth. Pour over the chicken. Mix the cracker crumbs and butter in a bowl. Spoon over the layers. Sprinkle with the poppy seeds. Bake at 375 degrees for 30 minutes.

Heather Elwood Watley

Dressed-Up Broccoli

Serves 8 to 10

1 (16-ounce) package frozen broccoli cuts, cooked and drained
8 ounces Velveeta cheese, cut into small pieces
1 cup crushed butter crackers
1/4 cup (1/2 stick) margarine, melted

Layer the broccoli and cheese in a 2-quart baking dish. Sprinkle with the cracker crumbs. Drizzle with the margarine. Bake at 350 degrees for 25 to 30 minutes or until bubbly and heated through.

Kelly Flournoy Pridgen

Crabby Cakes

Makes 20

1 pound crab meat, shells removed and crab meat flaked
3 tablespoons lemon juice
1 1/2 cups (6 ounces) shredded mozzarella cheese
3 ribs celery, chopped
1 (6-ounce) package stuffing mix
3/4 cup water
1/3 cup mayonnaise

Combine the crab meat, lemon juice, cheese, celery, stuffing mix, water and mayonnaise in a bowl and mix well. Chill for 20 minutes. Heat a large skillet over medium-low heat. Spray the skillet with nonstick cooking spray. Shape the crab meat mixture by 1/3 cupfuls into patties. Cook in the hot skillet for 3 to 5 minutes on each side or until golden brown.

Kelly Flournoy Pridgen

Campfire Baked Beans

Serves 4

1 (16-ounce) can baked beans	1 tablespoon vinegar
3 dashes of ketchup	4 slices bacon
1/4 cup packed brown sugar	

Combine the beans, ketchup, brown sugar and vinegar in a bowl and mix well. Spoon into a 1-quart baking dish. Top with the bacon. Bake at 300 degrees for 1 hour.

Meredith Lovein King

Garlic Green Beans

Serves 8

1/2 cup (1 stick) butter or margarine	4 (14-ounce) cans cut
1/2 cup packed brown sugar	green beans, drained
1/2 teaspoon minced garlic	Salt and pepper to taste
4 dashes of soy sauce	

Melt the butter in a saucepan. Stir in the brown sugar, garlic and soy sauce. Place the beans in a 9×13-inch baking dish. Pour the butter mixture over the beans. Bake at 350 degrees for 30 to 40 minutes or until heated through. Sprinkle with salt and pepper.

Mara Hall Kelly

Mr. McGregor's Favorite Cabbage

Serves 8

1 cup chopped onion
1 teaspoon olive oil
3 cups cornflakes
1/2 cup (1 stick) butter or margarine, melted
3 cups shredded cabbage
1 (8-ounce) can sliced water chestnuts, drained

1 1/2 cups (6 ounces) shredded Cheddar cheese
1 (10-ounce) can cream of celery soup
1 cup milk
1/2 cup mayonnaise

Sauté the onion in the olive oil in a skillet until soft. Mix the cornflakes and butter in a bowl. Spread one-half of the cornflake mixture in a 9×13-inch baking dish. Layer the cabbage, water chestnuts, sautéed onion and cheese over the cornflake mixture. Mix the soup, milk and mayonnaise in a bowl and spread over the layers. Top with the remaining cornflake mixture. Bake at 350 degrees for 45 minutes.

Note: Low-fat milk and soup can be used.

Mara Hall Kelly

Mom's Corn Soufflé

Serves 8

This is one of my mother's "staple" recipes that I grew up with. I have passed it around and around and around and think of her every time I make it.

2 eggs, beaten
1/4 cup (1/2 stick) butter or margarine, melted
1 cup sour cream
1 (14-ounce) can cream-style corn

1 (16-ounce) can whole kernel corn, drained
1 (9-ounce) package corn muffin mix
1 1/2 cups (6 ounces) shredded Cheddar cheese

Combine the eggs, butter, sour cream, cream-style corn, whole kernel corn and corn muffin mix in a bowl and mix well. Spoon into a 9×13-inch glass baking dish. Bake at 350 degrees for 30 to 35 minutes or until the center tests done and the top is light golden brown. Sprinkle with the cheese. Bake until the cheese melts.

Dradyn Coolik Hinson

Mozzarella Tomato Bake

Serves 4

2 plum tomatoes
1 tablespoon extra-virgin olive oil
1 tablespoon dried basil
Shredded mozzarella cheese to taste

Cut the tomatoes into halves lengthwise. Place cut side up in a baking dish and drizzle with the olive oil. Sprinkle with the basil and cheese. Bake at 350 degrees for 20 minutes or until the cheese is bubbly and light brown.

Wendy Ryan Gay

Very Veggie Casserole

Serves 8 to 10

To make a lower-calorie dish, use light mayonnaise, reduced-fat butter crackers, and 2 percent cheese.

1 (16-ounce) package frozen mixed vegetables
1 cup mayonnaise
1 small onion, chopped
1 cup (4 ounces) shredded Cheddar cheese
1 sleeve butter crackers, crushed
6 tablespoons butter, melted

Cook the mixed vegetables using the package directions; drain. Add the mayonnaise, onion and cheese and mix well. Spoon into a baking dish. Mix the cracker crumbs with the butter in a bowl. Sprinkle over the vegetable mixture. Bake at 350 degrees for 30 minutes.

Beth Lewis Williams

Yummy, Yummy Fruit Salad

Serves 12

Use any leftovers to make a fruit smoothie.

1 (20-ounce) can peach pie filling
1 (16-ounce) can mandarin oranges, drained
1 (16-ounce) can pineapple chunks, drained
2 (10-ounce) packages frozen strawberries, thawed and drained
3 bananas, sliced

Mix the pie filling, oranges, pineapple and strawberries in a bowl. Stir in the bananas just before serving.

Emily Braswell Trotter

Crispy Kaleidoscope Eggs

Makes 2 dozen

3 tablespoons butter
2$1/2$ cups crisp rice cereal
2 cups fruit-flavored cereal rings
3 cups miniature marshmallows
$1/2$ cup jelly beans

Place the butter in a large microwave-safe bowl. Microwave on High for 1 minute or until melted. Add the cereal, cereal rings, marshmallows and jelly beans. Microwave for 1 minute. Stir gently to mix without crushing the cereal. Cool for 2 minutes or until easy to handle. Butter your hands well and shape $1/4$ cup of the mixture at a time into the shape of an egg and place on a serving plate. The mixture will stay moldable for about 10 minutes.

Note: The eggs can be wrapped in clear plastic wrap for Easter baskets or school treats. The mixture also can be shaped as desired.

Nataly Maris Morgan

Reindeer Cookies

Makes 1 dozen

*These are fun to make for Santa and remember to
leave him a big glass of milk.*

1 (16-ounce) package refrigerator
peanut butter cookie dough or
sugar cookie dough
1/4 cup all-purpose flour

12 red "M & M's" Chocolate Candies
24 any color "M & M's" Chocolate Candies
24 small pretzel twists

Mix the cookie dough with the flour in a bowl to give the dough a stiffer consistency. Roll the
dough 1/4 inch thick on a lightly floured surface. Cut into twelve smooth-edged triangles or cut with
a bell-shaped cookie cutter. Place a red candy on the small tip of each triangle or the top of the bell
for the reindeer's nose. Place two other colors of the candy for the eyes on each one. Place a pretzel
twist on each side of each cookie for the antlers. Place on a cookie sheet. Bake at 350 degrees for
10 minutes or until light brown around the edge. Remove from the oven and cool on the cookie sheet
for 1 to 2 minutes. Remove to a wire rack to cool completely.

Beth Lewis Williams

Monster Cookies

Makes 20 to 30

1/2 cup (1 stick) butter, softened
1 cup granulated sugar
1 cup plus 2 tablespoons packed
brown sugar
3 eggs
2 cups creamy peanut butter
3/4 teaspoon light corn syrup

3/4 teaspoon vanilla extract
41/2 cups quick-cooking oats
2 teaspoons baking soda
1/4 teaspoon salt
1 cup "M & M's" Chocolate Candies
1 cup (6 ounces) semisweet
chocolate chips

Cream the butter, granulated sugar and brown sugar in the bowl of a stand mixer fitted with
a paddle attachment. Add the eggs, peanut butter, corn syrup and vanilla and beat well. Add the oats,
baking soda and salt and mix well. Stir in the candies and chocolate chips. Drop by spoonfuls onto
greased cookie sheets. Bake at 350 degrees for 10 to 15 minutes or until brown. Cool on wire racks.

Anna Skiles Muir, Atlanta, Georgia

Cupcakes with Icing

Makes 3 dozen

Cupcakes
3 1/2 cups cake flour
2 cups sugar
1 tablespoon baking powder
1/2 teaspoon salt
1 cup (2 sticks) butter, softened
1 cup milk
1 teaspoon vanilla extract
8 egg whites

Chocolate Icing
2 cups sugar
2 ounces unsweetened chocolate
1/2 cup (1 stick) margarine
1/2 cup milk
1/2 teaspoon vanilla extract

Vanilla Icing
1/2 cup (1 stick) butter, softened, or
    4 teaspoons milk
8 ounces cream cheese, softened
1 teaspoon vanilla extract or almond extract
1 (1-pound) package confectioners' sugar

For the cupcakes, mix the first four ingredients in a mixing bowl. Add the butter, milk and vanilla. Beat at medium speed for 1 minute. Beat in the egg whites one at a time. Beat for 1 minute longer. Beat at high speed for 2 minutes, scraping the side of the bowl. Fill greased paper-lined muffin cups two-thirds full. Bake at 350 degrees for 20 to 25 minutes or until a wooden pick inserted into the centers comes out clean. Cool in the pan for 15 minutes. Remove to a wire rack to cool completely. Spread with one of the icings.

For chocolate icing, cook the sugar, chocolate, margarine and milk in a saucepan over medium heat until the sugar dissolves. Bring to a boil and boil for 1 minute. Remove from the heat. Stir in the vanilla. Cool and beat until creamy. For vanilla icing, cream the butter and cream cheese in a mixing bowl. Add the vanilla and confectioners' sugar and beat until smooth.

Rainer Webb Mullin

Harvest Cupcakes

Makes 2 dozen

1 (2-layer) package spice cake mix
1 (16-ounce) can pumpkin
3/4 cup water

Combine the cake mix, pumpkin and water in a bowl and mix well. Spoon into miniature muffin cups sprayed with nonstick cooking spray. Bake at 350 degrees for 25 minutes.

Beth Lewis Williams

Magic Cookie Squares

Makes 4 to 5 dozen

3 cups graham cracker crumbs
1 cup (2 sticks) margarine, melted
2 (14-ounce) cans sweetened condensed milk
2 cups (12 ounces) semisweet chocolate chips
1 (10-ounce) package peanut butter chips
1 (7-ounce) package flaked coconut

Mix the graham cracker crumbs and margarine in a bowl. Press into an 11×18-inch baking pan. Spread the condensed milk evenly over the top. Sprinkle with the chocolate chips, peanut butter chips and coconut. Bake at 350 degrees for 30 minutes or until bubbles appear on the surface. Remove from the oven and cool completely. Cut into squares.

Lisa Spafford Brown

Cinnamon Muffins

Makes 2 dozen

1 (2-layer) package yellow cake mix
1 (6-ounce) package vanilla instant pudding mix
4 eggs
3/4 cup vegetable oil
3/4 cup water
Cinnamon-sugar to taste

Combine the cake mix, pudding mix, eggs, oil and water in a mixing bowl and mix until smooth. Fill paper-lined muffin cups one-third full. Sprinkle with cinnamon-sugar. Continue to fill with the remaining batter. Sprinkle the tops with cinnamon-sugar. Bake at 350 degrees for 10 to 15 minutes or until brown.

Joy Bowick Wells

Monkey See, Monkey Do Bread

Serves 6 to 8

1 loaf frozen yeast bread dough 1 cup chopped pecans (optional)
2 cups sugar 1 cup (2 sticks) butter, melted
2 tablespoons cinnamon

Cut the bread dough into 1-inch pieces and shape into balls. Mix the sugar and cinnamon in a bowl. Place the pecans in a bundt pan. Dip the dough balls in the butter and coat with the cinnamon-sugar. Place in the prepared pan. Let rise for 30 minutes using the bread dough package directions. Bake using the bread dough package directions. Remove from the oven and invert onto a serving platter large enough to cover all edges of the bundt pan.

Note: The bread will be gooey.

Heather Elwood Watley

Chocolate Chip Banana Muffins

Makes 1 to 1¹/2 dozen

1¹/2 cups all-purpose flour 3/4 cup sugar
1 teaspoon baking powder 1/3 cup butter, melted
1 teaspoon baking soda 3 or 4 bananas, mashed
1/2 teaspoon salt 1 cup (6 ounces) semisweet
1 egg chocolate chips

Mix the flour, baking powder, baking soda and salt in a large bowl. Combine the egg, sugar, butter and bananas in a bowl and mix well. Add to the flour mixture and mix well. Stir in the chocolate chips. Spoon into greased muffin cups. Bake at 375 degrees for 20 to 25 minutes or until brown.

Marietta Rushton O'Neill

Popsicles

Makes a variable amount

1 (3-ounce) package favorite flavor gelatin
2 cups boiling water
1/2 cup sugar
2 cups fruit juice the same flavor as the gelatin

Dissolve the gelatin in the boiling water in a bowl. Add the sugar and stir until dissolved. Stir in the juice. Pour into desired molds. Freeze for 8 to 10 hours or until firm.

Lisa Spafford Brown

Banana Pudding

Serves 8

3 egg yolks
1/2 cup sugar
1/2 teaspoon vanilla extract
12/3 cups milk
2 tablespoons cornstarch
3 egg whites, at room temperature
6 tablespoons sugar
1/2 teaspoon vanilla extract
1 (12-ounce) package vanilla wafers
4 ripe bananas

Combine the egg yolks, 1/2 cup sugar, 1/2 teaspoon vanilla, the milk and cornstarch in a double boiler. Cook over boiling water for 5 minutes or until thickened, stirring constantly.

To make the meringue, beat the egg whites in a mixing bowl until soft peaks form. Add 6 tablespoons sugar and 1/2 teaspoon vanilla gradually, beating until stiff peaks form.

Reserve 10 or 12 vanilla wafers for garnish. Layer the remaining vanilla wafers, pudding and bananas one-half at a time in a buttered 1-quart baking dish. Spread the meringue over the surface, sealing to the edges. Bake at 350 degrees for 10 to 12 minutes or until brown. Garnish with the reserved vanilla wafers. Cool slightly or chill before serving.

Susan Cashwell Pitts

Palatable Pairs for Keeping It Simple

Sit Back and Relax

Any of these entrées can be paired with a tossed salad for a simplified supper.
Try mixing an assortment of greens such as arugula, spinach, butter lettuce,
or romaine lettuce with a soft cheese, a few nuts, and toasted pita chips.
We recommend any of the accompanying salad dressings.

Entrées

Chicken and Spinach Lasagna	150	140	Spaghetti Pie
Comfort Beef Stew	136	137	Sweet T's Black Bean Enchiladas
Crepes aux Champignons	162	149	Firehouse Chicken and Dumplings
Basic Meatballs	139	79	Classic Vichyssoise
Salmon Piccata	160	76	Italian Chicken Soup
Gourmet Chicken and Herb Pizza	147	50	Easy Eggs Benedict
Sausage and Pasta Bake	145	52	Quiche à la Crab

Spicy Thousand Island Dressing

Serves 6 to 8

2 cups mayonnaise
1 tablespoon ketchup
1 tablespoon sweet pickle relish
1 teaspoon lemon juice
1/2 teaspoon chili powder
Dash of Worcestershire sauce
Freshly cracked pepper to taste

Combine the mayonnaise, ketchup, relish, lemon juice, chili powder, Worcestershire sauce and pepper in a bowl and mix well. Chill until serving time.

Lemon Vinaigrette

Serves 6

11/4 cups extra-virgin olive oil
1/2 cup plus 2 tablespoons fresh lemon juice
2 tablespoons chopped fresh basil
11/2 teaspoons white truffle oil
1 garlic clove, minced
1/2 teaspoon sugar
Salt and pepper to taste

Whisk the olive oil, lemon juice, basil, truffle oil, garlic, sugar, salt and pepper in a bowl until blended. Chill until serving time.

Creamy Dill Dressing

Serves 6

4 1/2 tablespoons sour cream
3 tablespoons mayonnaise
2 tablespoons horseradish
2 tablespoons finely chopped fresh dill weed
1 tablespoon olive oil
2 1/4 teaspoons white wine vinegar
1 teaspoon fresh lemon juice
Salt and freshly cracked pepper to taste

Whisk the sour cream, mayonnaise, horseradish, dill weed, olive oil, vinegar, lemon juice and pepper in a bowl until blended. Chill until serving time.

Orange Basil Vinaigrette

Serves 8 to 10

1/2 cup canned no-salt-added chicken broth
1/2 cup fresh orange juice
2 tablespoons white wine vinegar
1 tablespoon Dijon mustard
1 teaspoon cornstarch
1/2 teaspoon minced garlic
1/8 teaspoon salt
1 teaspoon minced fresh basil
1/4 teaspoon grated orange zest

Mix the broth, orange juice, vinegar, Dijon mustard and cornstarch in a small saucepan. Bring to a boil, stirring constantly. Cook for 1 minute. Remove from the heat. Mash the garlic and salt in a small bowl with the back of a spoon to form a paste. Add the orange juice mixture, basil and orange zest and mix well. Chill, covered, until serving time.

Note: The vinaigrette may be stored in the refrigerator for up to one week.

Rajun Cajun Vinaigrette

Serves 6 to 8

1 egg, lightly beaten
3 tablespoons Creole mustard
3 tablespoons Worcestershire sauce
1 1/2 teaspoons Tabasco sauce
2 teaspoons horseradish
1 teaspoon minced fresh garlic
1 teaspoon salt
1 teaspoon freshly ground pepper
1/4 cup (1 ounce) grated Parmesan cheese
1/3 cup apple cider vinegar
1/2 cup vegetable oil
1/2 cup extra-virgin olive oil

Blend the egg, Creole mustard, Worcestershire sauce, Tabasco sauce, horseradish, garlic, salt, pepper, cheese, vinegar, vegetable oil and olive oil in a bowl. Chill until serving time.

Note: If you are concerned about using raw eggs, use eggs pasteurized in their shells, which are sold at some specialty food stores.

Roquefort Dressing

Serves 6 to 8

6 ounces Roquefort cheese,
at room temperature
2 cups good-quality mayonnaise
1/2 teaspoon celery salt
1/2 teaspoon onion salt
1/2 teaspoon garlic salt
1/2 cup buttermilk

Crumble the cheese into a bowl. Stir in the mayonnaise, celery salt, onion salt, garlic salt and buttermilk, leaving the dressing somewhat lumpy. Chill until serving time.

Special Thanks

The members of the Junior League of Columbus wish to express sincere appreciation to all who have contributed to *Pull up a Chair* by providing valuable assistance and expertise.

Cindy Alexander
Rennie Bickerstaff
Richard Bickerstaff
Janice Biggers
Sis and Jim Blanchard
Bill Bowick
Mary Boyd
Mary Bradley
Jeanie Bross
Bettye and Cecil Cheves
Mimi Childs
Columbus Corner Bakery
Country's Bar-B-Que
Rachel Crumbley and Callaway Gardens
Donna and Mike Culpepper
Philip Denson
Dinglewood Pharmacy
Cal Evans
Betsy and Frank Garrard
Tim Gregory
Dick Hagan and the National Infantry Museum

Mary Harcourt
Martha Hatcher
Sally Hatcher
Nancy Johnson and Wynnton Arts Academy
Allie Kent and the Springer Opera House
Mary Dana Knight
Frank Lumpkin
Margaret and John Martin
Margaret McCormick
Clara Middlebrooks
Susan Mitchell
Laura Patrick
Laura Porter
Ernie Smallman
The Blue J Barber Shop
The Columbus Steeplechase
The Columbus Public Library
Blake Voltz
Sally Walden
Lisa White
Margaret Zollo

We would also like to thank League members, families, and friends who have assisted us in the development of *Pull up a Chair*. It is our sincere hope that no one has been inadvertently omitted from the acknowledgments.

Pull up a Chair

Contributors

Amy Giuliano Adams
Kathryn Kinnett Adams
Cindy Lesley Alexander
Julie Smith Alexander
Dowe Bricken Allen
Lisa McMullen Allen
Jenifer Clifton Amos
Patti Paine Andrews
Eric Arceneaux
Cordy Wiley Arnold
Susanna Elizabeth Avery-Lynch
Marquin Conklin Barrett
Kimberly Howell Beck
Kay Stewart Berard
Oscar Leon Betts, Jr.
Lisa Thigpen Beyer
Amy Johnson Bickerstaff
Becky Nye Bickerstaff
Catherine Zimmerman Bickerstaff
Fitzgerald Dunn Bickerstaff
Hugh Jefferson Bickerstaff, Jr
SaSa Walden Bickerstaff
Shannan Hartley Bickerstaff
Walker Reynolds (Rennie) Bickerstaff
William Boon Bickerstaff
Olivia Cheves Blanchard
Shelly Mathews Blanton
Susan Davis Bock
Mary Dell Borneman
Charlotte Lee Bowman
Mary Sprouse Boyd
Stacey Lamberth Boyd
Lu Ann Binns Brandon
Laurie Nester Brinegar
Lauren Brazil Briscoe
Jeanie Hinson Bross
Karan Cargill Brown
Lisa Spafford Brown
Lunday Brooks Buffington
Helen Jackson Burgin

Mary Tippins Cain
Betsy Wellman Calhoun
Wendy Kay Calhoun
Marcel Carles
Resa Pate Carter
Melissa Lipham Cason
Kristi Kimmell Casto
Michelle Moorman Caves
Abby Herndon Church
Gardiner Zollo Church
Hilda Hughes Church
Margaret Glenn Church
William Lanier (Putt) Church
Katie Taylor Coakley
Bernadette Bowick Coker
Leita Trammell Coleman
Kate Sievert Cook
Jennifer Dunn Cooley
Sandy Tally Coolik
Jennifer Wright Cooper
Betty Turner Corn
Shirley Monacelli Kurtz Craddock
Carolyn Zollo Crenshaw
Kathy Ward Culpepper
Robert M. Culver, Jr
Martha King Cunningham
Beth Rauch Cutshall
Jennifer Gillespie Daniel
Julie Davenport Davis
Launa Rodgers DesPortes
Sara Hatcher Dismuke
Jamie Donegan
Alice Gentry Douglas
Cortney Lynch Douglas
Mary Frances Calhoun Driver
Courtenay Toole Dykes
Jane Durden Etheridge
Edie Pendleton Evans
Mildred Sweat Evans
Sara Stola Evans

Contributors

Shari Phipps Evans
Carol Turner Flournoy
Jennifer Corradino Flournoy
Mary Elizabeth Flournoy
Virginia Newton Fuller
Claudia Sessions Garrard
Debbie Giglio Garrett
Wendy Ryan Gay
Cissy Carles Giglio
Marie Whisenhunt Gill
Kathleen Wren Gilliam
Susan Cheney Gilliam
Jennifer Hartley Glover
Timothy George Gregory, Jr
Christopher Brian Grier
Rachel Anne Grier
Robin Alexander Grier
Elizabeth Chambliss Gross
Mary Lynn Pugh Grubb
Jamie Gruber
Elvis (Kip) Hammersley, Jr.
Donna Sears Hand
Eleanor Glenn Hardegree
William Bryan Hardegree, III
Jennifer Daniel Harper
Brittany Locklar Harris
James Harris
Mallory Perkins Harris
Jessica DeLuca Hart
Martha Gilliam Hatcher
Sally Bickerstaff Hatcher
Libby McGill Hattaway
Cathy Powell Hemmings
Lenore Abbott Hilbert
Dradyn Coolik Hinson
Julie Hattaway Hinson
Patty Mudter Hobbs
Leslie Marie Holloway
Teresa Carswell Howard
Libby Carter Hudson

Michelle Williams Hudson
Nell Higdon Hudson
Jean Dudley Illges
Kathryn Fussell Jackson
Mitzi McCann Jackson
Mitchell Jarrett
Maggie Victoria Johnston
Dori Sponcler Jones
Jerry Floyd Jones
Pat Hurst Jordan
Jamie Keating
Mara Hall Kelly
Charleton Young Kennon
Lee Schomburg Kent
Maria Sandri Kent
Erwin Davidson Key
Charles Earnest Kimbrough
Meredith Lovein King
Helen Neal Kleiber
Mary Dana Huntley Knight
Crawford Pate Knox
Ginny Hendrix Lawrence
Cora Copelan Lee
Elicia Hindsman Maholick
Cammy Diaz Marchetti
Kathy Ann Martin
Charlene Roberts Marx
Katherine Ramsey Maxey
Frances Culver McConnell
Margaret Bradley McCormick
Edith Harwell McCullough
Lally Hutto McGurk
Kelly Bladen McKinstry
Elaine Tribble McMillen
Jensen Mast Melton
Joyce Mickle
Clara Turner Middlebrooks
Joannie Siano Minter
Susan Hickey Mitchell
Jennifer Annette Mordic

Contributors

Merle Cauthen Morgan
Nataly Maris Morgan
Anna Skiles Muir
Rainer Webb Mullin
Jenny Gardner Nobes
Marian Norman
Lee Lancaster Norred
Marietta Rushton O'Neill
Jennings Adams DeWitt Palmer
Mattie West Paris
Katie Giddens Parker
Joseph Carson Patrick
Laura Schomburg Patrick
Millie Peacock Patrick
Barbara Brettel Peacock
Mary Helen Peacock
Allison Weaver Peak
Anne Hayes Drinkard Pearce
Betty Rainey Pearson
Whitney Rice Pease
Julie McCullough Pendleton
Meg Pyles Perkins
Susan Cashwell Pitts
John Kirkland Pope
Kelly Flournoy Pridgen
Laura Leggett Raines
Mia Knighton Rice
Marci Richardson
Margie Thrasher Richardson
Corrin Wellons Riley
Kathy Johnson Riley
Sandra Rodgers
Meghan Kennedy Rumer
Colleen Day Rustin
Margie Lacy Saunders
Susan Carroll Schlader
Hadley Upchurch Scott
Fran Martin Sessions
Sarah Hart Sillitto
Sarah Linne Sluder

Mary King Smalley
Ernest Smallman IV
Louise Tennent Smith
Mollie Morton Smith
Lela Morgan Snead
Britney Vickers Stahl
Barbara Hamby Swift
Cary Taylor
Nell Louise Taylor
Beth Foster Thomas
Shriver Jones Tommey
Emily Braswell Trotter
Dell McMath Turner
Sue Marie Thompson Turner
Lee Helton Tyra
Amella Alcorn Vaught
Blakely Hanes Voltz
Donna Eskew Voynich
Mitchi McKnight Wade
Sally Kimbrough Walden
Katie Heard Waldrep
Jennifer Ellington Walker
Margaret Marston Ward
Melinda Moon Ward
Heather Elwood Watley
Candice Lamare Wayman
Joy Bowick Wells
Lisa Lane White
Tami Sparks Whitehead
Beth Lewis Williams
Chris Wagner Williams
Tiffany Kitchens Wilson
Christopher Stevenson Woodruff
Chloe Mason Wynn
Margaret Glenn Zollo

Index

Index

Index

Pull up a Chair

Index

Pull up a Chair

Index

To order additional copies of

Pull up a Chair

southern company, conversations & cuisine

or to order

A Southern Collection Then and Now

contact

Junior League of Columbus, Georgia, Inc.
700 Broadway • Columbus, GA 31901
Web site: jlcolumbus.com
Telephone: 706.327.4207 • Fax: 706.327.4430